CW01651626

Planning your Marquee Wedding

Planning your Marquee Wedding

The Ultimate Guide

Emily Andrew

Planning Your Marquee Wedding
Copyright © Emily Andrew 2021

Published by Compass-Publishing UK
ISBN 978-1-913713-77-5

Edited and typeset by The Book Refinery Ltd
www.thebookrefinery.com

Photography © Andy Davison Photography
Cover photo by © Andy Davison Photography
Photos of Emily Andrew © Andrew Kahumbu Photography
Illustrations © Jon Hooper. All rights reserved 2021.

The right of Emily Andrew to be identified as the author of this work has been asserted in accordance with the Copyright, Designs and Patents Act, 1988.

All rights reserved. No part of this publication may be reproduced, stored in a retrieval system, or transmitted, in any form or by any means (electronic, mechanical, photocopying, recording or otherwise), without the prior written permission of the publisher.

The author and publishers do not assume and hereby disclaim any liability to any party for any loss, damage or disruption allegedly arising from any information or suggestions in this book. Readers are encouraged to do their own due diligence and put in place their own risk assessments and health and safety precautions relevant to their own wedding plans.

A CIP catalogue record for this book is available from the British Library.

Printed and bound by CMP Print, Dorset UK.

Dedicated to all the new brides!

Contents

Section 2 - The Practical Stuff

63

Section 3 - Designing Your Marquee

105

Welcome!

Hi! I'm so excited to have you here, so I can share my favourite type of wedding with you: marquee weddings! As a professional wedding planner, specialising in marquees and dry-hire venues in the beautiful county of Norfolk, UK, I have over nine years' experience creating stunning wedding venues in what is literally an empty field. I completely understand how much work and planning is involved in creating a marquee wedding, but I also know how daunting it can be for someone who has never done it before (and let's face it, that's most brides and grooms!). So I'm here with loads of handy hints, tips, advice and explanations to take you from being confused to being in control of planning your own such wedding. From what makes a perfect marquee site, all the way through to the schedule of timings for your big day, you'll find this book answers all the niggly questions you have and even some you don't yet know you have!

Here in the UK, there's a variety of marquee-based weddings, whether you're booking a venue that has its own marquee, a dry-hire venue that has space for you to put up your own marquee for the duration of your hire, or a marquee to put on private land (for example, if you have a big enough garden, a paddock or a field that you're planning on using). Throughout this book, my main focus will be on weddings on private land.

TF 4 AF
M J ROLLS

Section 1

WHERE TO START

Marquees are the perfect blank canvas.

Create a stress-free, memorable wedding day.

Why Are Marquee Weddings So Special?

For any of you who aren't sure if this could be an option for you, then here are my five reasons why I *love* a marquee wedding, and why it could be the perfect choice for you.

1. Choice

When it comes to this type of wedding, you have masses of choice! Broadly speaking, you get to choose everything, as it's a pop-up event space, so the whole thing is selected and chosen by you. This will start with the address your marquee will be installed at, going through to the timings of your day, the style of the marquee you wish to hire, its size, its finish, and all the fittings and fixtures within it.

In terms of your day, you'll get the maximum amount of choice with a marquee – there are far fewer restrictions on your wedding day than at any other style of venue (think elastic walls, you can have long tables or round tables, and you're not restricted by a venue's schedule). If you have set ideas and are struggling to find a bricks-and-mortar wedding venue that will provide it, then a marquee is probably going to fulfil your needs.

2. FLEXIBILITY

Because you're bringing everything you need for your wedding day onto the marquee site, you have masses of flexibility. You'll have more adjustability with your number of guests, the start and end times of your day, and with the suppliers you commission to deliver your day. Many wedding venues will dictate the start and end times of your wedding (often due to legal restrictions), and they'll offer packages for your food and drink, and for the furniture you must use, whereas with a marquee, you have the ability to pick all of these things. Wedding venues often have a preferred-supplier list, which may be commission based, and they'll encourage you to choose your suppliers from this list (and in some cases, you absolutely have to select your suppliers from their list).

If your number of guests fluctuates, you'll also have the ability to expand or reduce the size of a marquee to accommodate them, so you'll only be paying for the space you need. It can often be a real problem to get the number of guests confirmed, and this is less of an issue with a marquee.

Also, some venues will offer food-and-drinks packages for your whole wedding day – from the reception canapés through to evening food and everything in between – and having a marquee means you don't have these restrictions, so you'll have more options in catering for your guests.

3. BUDGET

As I mentioned previously, with the benefits of flexibility and choice that this style of wedding offers, you can control your budget more carefully. You'll only hire items you actually need, and you can pick the style and size of marquee that fits your budget. Through having the ability to pick the suppliers you want to work with, you'll be able to select suppliers that fit your budget and will provide the exact service you require. One of the biggest expenses of a wedding is the venue, and although marquee weddings are not a cheap option, you'll have lots more options – from the marquee to the food, drink, décor and entertainment – which will help to keep your expenditure in check.

4. LOCATION

Basically, marquees can go almost anywhere! If you love the outdoors, then a marquee maximises the best of your wedding's surroundings. With panoramic windows, you can have the most amazing views of the countryside or estate on which it's sited. Most brides and grooms who pick marquees love the fact that they can bring the outside into the marquee, and if the weather is fine enough, the whole marquee becomes the outside; with the side walls pulled back, the unadulterated views will mean you can really be at one with your surroundings.

Marquees can also be great add-on spaces to existing venues, so if you need a room extension, then bolt a marquee onto the outside, and simply extend the room seamlessly to create extra celebration space.

5. PERSONALISATION

Marquees offer the ultimate blank canvas for an event. Unlike bricks-and-mortar venues, marquees can be in a variety of shapes to create the space that will offer you and your guests the best event experience. Being a blank canvas, you can personalise every element of your day completely to make your wedding day totally unique to you. I love the fact that each marquee becomes a representation of one of my couples and their personalities. You have *complete freedom* to personalise everything from carpets and linens to your bar menu and timings. Your guests will get to experience your wedding day exactly how you want it to be, complete with all your personal touches.

I've created this book to give you some insider tips and a structure for your own wedding-planning journey. Marquee weddings are brilliant, but they do have their own set of complexities. I'm going to take you step by step through the things you must consider, so you can plan your own wedding like a pro!

Good luck and happy planning!

Step-by-Step Guide to Planning Your Wedding

You're probably new to all of this, so I thought it might be helpful if I gave you a bit of an overview of where to start when planning your wedding in general terms.

What time of year would you like to get married?

Each season has its own positives and negatives, which you'll need to consider when planning your wedding. For example, a winter wedding can be beautifully romantic, but you'll want to pick a venue that can be cosy and reachable in any weather conditions. With a summer wedding, you can really make the most of the weather and plan parts of your day outside.

Wedding date

Once you know roughly when you want to get married, set a date. Bear in mind the season, as I mentioned previously, but also what's achievable from a financial perspective. If you're going to have to save money each month to pay for your wedding, consider how long this may take to get a pot of money big enough to fund your big day. Don't put yourself under unnecessary stress from this; your wedding should be memorable for all the right reasons, not for making you prematurely grey! If you have your heart set on a specific date then bear in mind the popularity of peak summer dates.

BUDGET

Deciding between you both what you feel comfortable spending on your wedding is a good starting point for drawing up a budget. It's really important that you set yourself a budget at the start of the planning process, so you can try to manage your finances. There are two ways of doing this: you can either start with the total amount you wish to spend and then divide it up into categories, or you can start by deciding what you want to spend by category and see how it totals up. The second option is likely to result in a bigger budget than calculating it the first way!

At this stage, it's also important to work out roughly where your priorities lie; for example, if you're both foodies, then you may decide it would be a wiser move for you to save money on, say, flowers, to allow you to apportion more money to your catering. There's no right or wrong here, but you have to feel comfortable with the total amount you want to spend, and be realistic (though make sure you have a contingency fund for miscellaneous items!). Don't start your married life with a huge debt just from one day!

Later in the book, in the *Making the Most of Your Money* chapter (page 53), I also talk about how you can save money (or splurge).

Prioritise your guest list to include your most favourite people.

GUEST LIST

This is bound to be a contentious area, especially if you've got kind parents giving you money to pay for your special day! It's worth thinking about how many people you want to be there to celebrate with you, because this will help narrow down what size of marquee you'll need. Also bear in mind who's on your guest list; try asking yourself some simple questions, such as determining who has supported you both in your lives up to this point, who would you not miss being there (sometimes this is a hard call, but when you're paying per head for each guest, costs mount up quickly), who you'll still be friends with in five/twenty year's time, and whether work colleagues are classed as your nearest and dearest.

Drawing up a guest list may also highlight other issues you must consider in the later stages of your planning, such as travel arrangements, accommodation arrangements or disabled access.

Another massive issue with guest lists can be children – do you invite them or not? Primarily, this issue can be resolved by answering these questions:

1. Do you have any children of your own who'll be there?

2. Do any of your close family / wedding party have any children whom you wish to attend?

If the answer to both these questions is no, then my advice would be to not invite children. Just make it very clear on the invitations, and perhaps have a chat with your guests before you even send out the invitations to gauge their reactions; after all, you don't want this to upset people, but it is *your* wedding day.

Ceremony

Do you want your wedding ceremony to be religious or not? That's going to be a big factor in the rest of your planning. If you do want to have a religious ceremony, then that will also be considered a legal ceremony if conducted at a registered religious building that's appropriate to your religion (please do check if the venue you wish to use is a registered religious building).

If you're not having a religious ceremony, then you'll need to think about whether you want to get married in a registry office or at a licensed venue for your wedding to be legally binding; in either case, the ceremony would be led by a registrar. If you choose a licensed venue, then you now have the option of saying your vows outside or inside, in what's referred to as a duo ceremony.

If you wish to have your main wedding celebration at a venue that is neither a religious building, a registry office nor a licensed venue, then it will be necessary to have a separate legal ceremony to your main celebration (generally done at the registry office before your main celebration) – assuming you want your wedding to be legal.

If you do have a separate legal ceremony or don't want a legal ceremony, you can opt for a celebrant-led ceremony. A celebrant-led ceremony isn't restricted like a registrar-led one is, so you have complete flexibility over location, timing and what vows you say to each other.

Location

Location is a big factor in the early stages of your planning; are you opting to have your wedding close to your family or where you live now (if these are different)? Quite often, I find that my clients choose to have their wedding where they grew up, which means most of their guests will be travelling specifically for their celebration. In this case, then why not extend your celebration over the whole weekend? In this way, you can make the most of the area your guests are travelling to and the extra time you'll have to catch up with everyone. Obviously, if you are thinking of hosting and catering for your guests over more than one day, then you'll need to factor this into your finances.

In terms of finding a marquee location, there are various places you can research:

» Fields advertised in online directories for use with marquees.

» Exclusive-use properties with ample outside space.

» Dry-hire venues.

» A local landowner who is willing to hire you their field.

» Venues that have space in their grounds for marquees.

BEST MEN AND WOMEN

As soon as you've decided on some of the details listed previously, it's certainly worth asking your planned groomsmen and bridesmaids whether they're prepared to be intrinsically involved in your big day. Your bridesmaids and groomsmen must be people who are prepared to assist you in your planning and to help make your day run smoothly. So often, I hear sad stories about the bride's friends, whom she has asked to be her bridesmaids, turning into complete prima donnas, demanding certain types of dresses, shoes, make-up, etc., and making the bride's life extra stressful and fraught with emotional dilemmas. The people you ask should appreciate that it's your wedding day and be honoured that you've selected them to take these important roles.

Venue

Last but certainly not least is your venue. It's wise to have an idea of the style of venue you want to hold your wedding at before you go headlong into planning. Assuming you do decide you're having a marquee wedding, you have various options for this, whether it's an exclusive-use venue, a dry-hire venue, a field, a garden or a paddock. I discuss the specifics of the marquee site next in this book, in the *Assessing Your Site* chapter (page 24).

If you nail these key things first, *then* you can get on to all the pretty stuff, and you'll find your planning is a lot smoother! If you decide to use the services of a professional wedding planner like me, then they'll guide you expertly through each of these steps.

Assessing Your Site

First things first: where's your wedding going to be and where are you putting up your marquee? Some of the main drivers behind your decision about a marquee will be the locations you have available to you (see the earlier *Location* segment on page 21) and the flexibility that this will give you in creating the wedding you actually want – not simply buying a wedding package with no personality and creativity.

Marquee Location and Ground Conditions

Where's your marquee going to go and what's the ground like? It's important to consider how the ground will be at the exact time of year you're planning your wedding. Is it sandy, muddy, becomes water-logged easily, bumpy, meadow grass, lawn, etc.? If you're lucky enough to have access to your site a year before your wedding, it's a great idea to really look at how the ground behaves and to get your chosen marquee company to do a survey of the site, as it'll give you a clearer picture of the costs involved and how the marquee will best fit.

SITE ACCESS

You'll also need to think about the *access for your site*; although most marquees aren't delivered on articulated lorries, you must still make provision for their turning circle, and make sure any entrances are wide enough for one to fit through, that any shrubbery isn't blocking access, and there aren't any low-hanging branches on trees. This applies to the whole site, not just the access point. Are there any weight limits on any bridges that may need to be crossed en route to your site from the marquee company's depot?

DOUBLE CHECKING THESE SORTS OF DETAILS AND MAKING PROVISIONS IF THEY'RE GOING TO CAUSE PROBLEMS, IS IMPERATIVE TO A SMOOTH-FLOWING, ON-TIME AND ON-BUDGET WEDDING.

GROUND PREPARATION

In addition, the ground will have to be prepared for any vehicles coming on site. For example, if it's very soft ground, then with the volume and weight of delivery vehicles entering the site, the entrance is likely to become very churned up and look unattractive. This is more of a significant problem if it's going to be where your guests enter as well, so consider either opening up a second guest entrance or preserving the ground with either heavy-duty matting or plastic track. The main factor that comes into play in considerations such as these will be whom the land belongs to. If it isn't your land, then there may be conditions set regarding how you use the land and the state that you must leave the ground in after your wedding.

If you're using a field or lawn, then you'll need to prepare the ground before your marquee is erected. This is something your marquee company can advise you on, but the key points are identifying where any *utilities' cables and pipework* are under your site, and cutting the grass and using a roller on it to make it as flat and firm as possible (this may need to be done more than once), so it's primed for the marquee. If you have official plans of the site, then you may have some details of where there's any cabling, which I'd certainly advocate showing to your marquee company during the site visit.

Other site options

In an ideal world, your marquee site will be a large, flat, open field, but there are *many other site options*. For example, if you're entertaining at home, but you don't quite have enough room, then a marquee can be butted onto the outside of your house to extend out from a room, increasing your seating capacity. You can get really clever with this and integrate it so well that the room flows seamlessly from the bricks-and-mortar room into the marquee structure.

Of course, marquees don't have to go straight onto unpaved ground, you can place clear span marquees onto tennis courts or other areas of *hardstanding*, as this type of marquee does not require pegging into the ground.

If you're planning on using your garden, then you may wish to build your marquee around *certain features* of your garden – such as a fountain, pond or flower bed – all of which are completely possible; you just need to plan your final layout and design around these focal points in an inclusive way. It's also possible to build marquees out onto open water or over a swimming pool. With the right sort of structural engineering and platform, this can really be quite awe-inspiring.

Parking

Parking for your guests is another key consideration. Is there enough space either on the marquee site or at a neighbouring location for all your guests to park? I also go into more detail later on in the *How to Make Sure Your Day Runs Smoothly* chapter (page 90), so do take note of this section too. You'll have to consider the ground of the parking area as well, because if it isn't hardstanding, then the grass could get ruined, especially if there's been rain in the lead up to your wedding. Think about the access your guests will have to the parking area: Is the entrance wide enough? Is there a decent line of sight from a safety point of view (this is especially important if they'll be turning onto a busy main road)? What's the journey like from the car park to the marquee site, if the parking is not on site? Will you be hiring in any minibuses or coaches to transport your guests? If so, then check that they'll be able to negotiate the entrance and that the ground is solid enough for them – no one wants a stuck coach!

You'll need to revise many of these points when you come to review your contingency plans for bad weather, but it's certainly worth bearing them in mind as early on in the planning as you can, so as to avoid any nasty surprises.

Above-site considerations

What's above your marquee site? If there are any overhead electrical cables or telephone wires that may cause an issue for the installation, you may have to adjust the orientation of your marquee within the site slightly so that there will be plenty of clearance for the marquee team to set it up safely. The guidelines state that any overhead cables must be 3m above the roof of the marquee. If you don't have the space to adjust the location of your marquee to avoid them, it's possible to contact the electrical supply company and ask them to put a sheath over the cables for protection. Overhanging branches may also present a concern if they obstruct the space needed for erecting the marquee.

It might be possible to chop away any offending branches, but double check your site not only with your marquee company but also with the landowner.

THE FLOW OF YOUR DAY

Think about how you want to use your marquee site to best effect. Consider the *flow of your day* and put yourself in the shoes of your guests. Where, how and when will they enter the marquee? Where will they be greeted with reception drinks? What views would you like your guests to have while they sit and enjoy your wedding breakfast (which is the first meal you share as a married couple, regardless of the time of day)? If you have amazing views on only one side of your marquee site, then maximising this by positioning it so that panoramic windows will give unadulterated views. There's a high likelihood that you'll have evening suppliers arriving on site after your guests are already there, so plan how those suppliers will access the site and where they'll unload to reduce the amount of disruption to your guests' enjoyment of your day.

You may also want to think about the direction of the sun when plotting where your marquee will sit on your site. If you have an open view from the marquee, it might be nice to be able to see the sunset through the side of your marquee that has the windows.

WHEN YOU BOUGHT THIS BOOK, YOU'LL HAVE RECEIVED A COPY OF MY CHECKLIST FOR YOUR MARQUEE SITE ASSESSMENT, WHICH WILL HELP YOU. OR IF I'M HELPING YOU WITH YOUR SPECIAL DAY, THEN I'LL TAKE CARE OF THIS FOR YOU.

*Here's your marquee site assessment checklist:**

Assessing Your Site

CHECKLIST

What you should consider:

- ☐ What is the ground like?
- ☐ Is the access wide enough for large vans / lorries?
- ☐ Is access to your site via any bridges with weight or height limits?
- ☐ Are there any low-hanging branches?
- ☐ Are there any overhead utility cables?
- ☐ What is under the ground (e.g. any gas / water pipes)?
- ☐ What preparations might you need to do to the ground (e.g. rolling or mowing)?
- ☐ What parking facilities are there?
- ☐ Do you have any neighbours you need to be mindful of (e.g. sound levels or extra traffic)?
- ☐ What is the view from the marquee?
- ☐ Where does the sun go down in relation to your marquee site?
- ☐ What space is there on your site for the catering tent, reception drinks area, etc.?
- ☐ Is there enough space for vehicles to turn around?
- ☐ Are there any structures / landscape features that need building around?

**Included in your checklist pack*

Different Styles of Marquees

The topic of marquees can get quite full of jargon, and different words can be used for the same thing. This section is intended to explain some of these terms to you.

The style of marquee you pick may depend on the time of year you wish to use it, the available space you have or the ground you're putting the marquee onto, as well as the aesthetic you're looking to achieve. The following will give you some ideas as to which may be the best marquee for your wedding.

Clear span marquee

The most common marquee style is a clear span or a framed marquee. This pretty much is what it says! It has no internal poles, simply the external framework, so you get a clear, fully open space to use how you wish. The other advantage of these is that they can be put on a solid surface because they're kept in place with weights, rather than requiring long metal stakes to be hammered into the soil. This means clear span marquees don't require any guy ropes, giving the additional benefit that they can fit directly into the available space with a smaller footprint.

Clear Span Marquee

You can easily bolt on catering tents, entrance porches or additional smaller marquees to create adjoining rooms. These are mainly made from white polyvinyl chloride (PVC), and they need an internal lining to hide the heavy-duty metal framework. Over the dance-floor area, you can add a black lining with twinkly, small lights embedded in it (called pea light linings or starlit canopies). You also can have a partially clear roof, which looks really stunning but does act very much like a greenhouse!

You can segment the large space with reveal curtains to keep part of the marquee out of sight until later in your day or use baffle screens to provide discreet entrances to the catering tent.

There's a lot of flexibility with a clear span marquee because you can simply increase the length by adding on extra panels.

These structures are also more suitable for all-year use. You can add proper lockable doors and glass windows into the framework for a more robust, semi-permanent style of structure (which is ideal if you're planning a winter wedding, as the heat won't escape as quickly). Clear span marquees are also sturdier than other types of marquee; when there are strong winds, they can be weighted down with water ballasts. These are tested to withstand wind speeds of up to 80mph!

Typically, clear span marquees have a wall height of 2.4m and bay widths of 3m, which join together to make up the length of the marquee. The width can vary, depending on the stock your marquee supplier has, but it can be anywhere from 9m up to 20m for a really specialist structure.

» These marquees are good for erecting on any type of surface.

» They are unsuitable for a rustic-style wedding.

Traditional marquee

A more traditional style of marquee is a pole tent. This is supported by a frame that includes king poles, which hold up the roof and sit in the middle of the marquee space. Large guy ropes and stakes keep this style of marquee upright, so you must allow for extra space round the outside of your marquee to accommodate them. The king poles can be a bit of a challenge to integrate into the overall design of your marquee, and generally speaking, it's not such a flexible space as a clear span marquee; for example, you can't install reveal curtains, and any bolted-on catering tents or porches do not join as seamlessly.

They do, however, provide an imposing silhouette and lend themselves to country-style weddings. These are usually made of a waterproof and breathable canvas, and they can be used without an internal lining for a more rustic style.

The size of a pole tent is limited as you can't bolt on additional panels with the same degree of flexibility as with a clear span marquee.

» These marquees are good for traditional-style weddings.

» They are unsuitable for segmenting the space into different areas.

A variation on a pole tent is a sailcloth-style marquee, which has curved ends and usually has wrap-around, panoramic windows for unobscured views.

Bedouin marquees are named as such because they resemble Arabian-style tents. They often come with printed-cotton linings, furniture and lighting that are in keeping with this style and theme. They're erected in the same way as a pole tent, but they're usually squarer with Arabian-style flourishes and finishing touches to the pelmets and canvas.

- These marquees are good for a more elegant, high-end-style wedding.
- They are unsuitable for creating your own style of wedding design, as the Arabian influences dictate the style more.

CHINESE HAT MARQUEE

Chinese hats, pagodas or pods can be hexagonal, rectangular or square. They're made from white PVC and have tall points to their roofs. The benefit of these is that they can be put anywhere – like a clear span – as their framework is similar. You can also bolt multiple ones together to create a unique and interesting space. They're great for dissecting your space into different areas, which is something that can otherwise be quite daunting with a large, open, rectangular marquee.

» These marquees are good for creating different spaces to celebrate in.

» They are unsuitable for a rustic-style wedding.

Chinese Hat Marquee

STRETCH MARQUEE

A contemporary style of marquee is a stretch marquee, which looks like one large piece of canvas that has been stretched across some internal king poles with the ends then taken down to the ground. They look quite unique, but you can create some special visual effects with clever uplighting and internal spotlights.

They're a bit of a challenge to join catering tents on to seamlessly, and they're a fairly standard size, so it's also harder to bolt on a porchway or any other annexe, which means you don't have the same flexibility as with a clear span.

» They're great for summer weather, though, because you can unzip all the sides to give unadulterated views of your surroundings.

» These marquees are good for making a statement.

» They are unsuitable for creating different spaces to celebrate in.

Stretch Marquee

TIPIS

Tipis are really popular, and they can be bolted together (in a similar way to the Chinese hats) to create a large space that isn't quite as open as a clear span or pole marquee, but that has bags of character. They're supported by a complex network of timber poles, which meet at a point in the middle of the ceiling. The poles look stunning and can be decorated with flowers, foliage or fairy lights to look really pretty. However, they do cut into the internal space you have available, and you'll need to be mindful of how you arrange your tables, as there will be height restrictions in some areas of the tipi. Another little quirk of a tipi is that you can put a fire pit inside one as there are roof vents, which is really cool, and it's great if the weather is slightly inclement, or for toasting marshmallows!

- » Tipis have a fairly space-hungry footprint and they're not as economical as clear span marquees.
- » These marquees are good if you have a minimal décor budget.
- » They are unsuitable for putting on any ground except grass.

Setting Your Budget

It's a challenge at the beginning because you don't know what you need to spend money on, and there are lots of costs. As an inexperienced marquee-wedding planner, it's a challenge to understand what you have to budget for. Here are the main costs associated with a marquee wedding.

Your Marquee

The first thing to include in your budget is an allocation for your marquee! This will be a large amount of your budget. Because marquees offer enormous flexibility, you could be spending anywhere from a few hundred up to thousands of pounds, but this will all depend on your number of guests, the style of marquee you choose and the time of year (for example, you'll need heating, solid flooring and proper doors if it's a winter wedding). Also, is there a site fee for the venue? Or are you lucky enough to have space at home or do you know a local farmer who will lend you his field?

There are then extra costs involved with a marquee; it's not just four sides and a roof!

When you do your site visit with your marquee company, they'll give you specific advice, but look at the condition of the ground. Will you have to put down hard flooring to even out a lumpy, bumpy site? Or if the site has quite peaty soil, then hard flooring can help to prevent excessive dampness rising up from the ground. What sort of lining do you want? Some marquees have beautiful, printed linings, but they'll push the budget up. Are you happy with the standard lighting your marquee company can provide, or are you looking for something with a little more of a wow factor?

Catering

Another large cost will be your catering, and this will vary greatly depending on your number of guests and the types of food and drink you wish to serve. The number of guests is a significant factor in this and not just from the point of view of a price per head, as you must also factor in the staffing and service costs; that is, the more guests you have, the more expensive your staffing bill from your caterers will be.

You'll also most likely require a field kitchen for your catering team, which must be the correct size and specification for them. For an average wedding, I find that a 6m x 6m catering tent with flooring and strip lighting is sufficient, but do check with your catering team, as they may have certain requirements themselves. The catering tent will need to be equipped, so budget for hiring ovens, hot cupboards, water boilers, tables, etc. Most of the specifics for this will depend on your final menu, but it's definitely advisable to factor something for this into your budget from the start.

You must include furniture for your marquee, and all glassware, linens, cutlery and crockery. The best thing to do is to go online and find a hire company, so you can just get a rough online estimate for the costs to pop in your budget. Some marquee companies will include furniture in their quotation, and some catering companies will provide linens and crockery, etc., but it varies massively, so my advice would always be to err on the side of caution and allow for it in your initial budget.

However, the joy of a marquee is that you can have whatever you'd like, so think fish-and-chip van, pasty van or a spit roast – literally anything is possible. Because you're completely in control, you can tailor your menu to fit your budget as well, ranging from £5 a head for a fish-and-chip supper up to hundreds of pounds per head for a fine-dining experience.

Furniture

The furniture you'll require comprises dining tables and chairs (assuming you're having a formal sit-down wedding breakfast), a table for your cake, a table for gifts, a drink-dispensing table, a dance floor, staging for your DJ or band, and perhaps a casual-seating area. We'll go into these finishing touches in more detail in due course.

But, if formal isn't your style, and you're having a more casual style of food, why not get creative and mix it up? You could forego having formally laid dining tables, and instead style your marquee entirely with poufs and sofas. Depending on your catering needs and style, this is your time to think outside the box.

Drink

If you're providing all alcoholic and soft drinks yourself, then you'll need to hire a dry bar for the drinks to be served from, plus you'll have to add into your budget the amount you wish to spend on alcohol. If you're opting for a pay bar, then this is a cost that your guests will bear. I explain more about your bar and drink options later in the book (see *The Finances* part in the *Bar Hire and TENs* chapter, page 74).

Utilities

> If you're literally building your wedding marquee in a field, then think about the utilities you'll require, such as water and a generator for the power.

The water factor will depend largely on the preferences of your catering team; for example, I have some caterers I work with who will only work where there's access to potable water, either from an outside tap or via a hose, and I have others who are happy to have water brought to site, whether this is via a large bowser or from multiple large water bottles.

You'll also need to hire portable toilets. Heating could be something you wish to consider including as well, depending on the time of year you're getting married. All of this is covered in more detail in *The Practical Stuff* section of this book, starting on page 63.

Think about how formal you want your place settings to be.

What might you need to include on your tables?

Edible or gluggable wedding favours are always a hit!

Insurance

Insurance is also something that you should pop into your budget, especially for marquees, as you'll have a lot of equipment on site. Don't forget that you must get insurance cover from the moment the marquee arrives on site to the point it's removed fully; that is, not just for your wedding day. There are a variety of insurance companies that specialise in wedding insurance, so just make sure you find a policy that covers a marquee specifically. When you hire your marquee, some marquee companies will automatically include a damage waiver in your hire fee, but always discuss this with them, along with what your own policy covers; in some cases, they may consider removing their damage waiver if your policy is robust enough. It's your responsibility to keep your marquee and site secure, which may be a challenge if it's in a field or meadow, so you may need to employ an overnight security team.

Lighting

Lighting is another area that must be included. Having some creative lighting inside your marquee can really elevate your space into a unique and beautiful environment. Lighting can also be a clever way of transforming your marquee space from an elegant daytime dining space into a fun and funky evening party space! There are the obvious lighting elements inside your marquee, but in addition, you'll need an allowance in your budget for external lighting. This could be for ornamental features, such as uplighting a tree or draping festoon lights along the outside of your marquee. You have to think about safety aspects as well, such as how guests will find their way in the dark to the toilets or the car park, and if there are any ditches or open water, then lighting can highlight dangerous areas that need to be avoided.

Ceremony

The legal side of your marriage will also need to be included in your overall budget; the fees for registrars, religious ceremonies or even celebrant-led services can all be found online. Don't forget to include any associated costs that come with your ceremony, such as transport for your guests (if you're providing it) between your marquee and your ceremony venue, orders of service, confetti, flowers and decorations for your ceremony (as already mentioned), and music for the ceremony itself.

Entertainment

You'll want to include entertainment in your budget, in the form of a band, DJ or any other artists who will be there for your day. There may be other suppliers you wish to bring in to help you run your day, such as a toastmaster or a wedding planner who offers on-the-day management, so don't forget to add those into your budget at this stage too.

Décor is an important part of personalising your day, and I'd include in this figure your flowers (the personal ones for the bridal party, plus the ceremony flowers and the flowers for the marquee), any wedding stationery, signage, candles and trimmings. There's a whole section dedicated to this subject, *Designing Your Marquee,* starting on page 105. Keeping tight control over this side is really important, as it can easily escalate out of control!

CONTINGENCY FUND

It's also advisable to consider having a contingency fund, and I'd recommend setting this as 5–10% of your total budget, just to cover any areas that end up being more expensive than you planned or to cover any additional costs that you weren't expecting.

THE EXTRAS

Other more general areas of expenses to take account of in your budget are your rings, hair and make-up for the bride and bridal party, dresses for the bride and bridesmaids, suits for the groom and his groomsmen, the honeymoon, accommodation, transport, and photography.

Picking Your Marquee Supplier

Picking your marquee supplier can be a tough decision to make. This is partly because they'll be asking you to secure their services without you actually having seen the end result of exactly what you'll be getting on your wedding day. Doing your due diligence and researching as much as possible before you pay your deposit is so important.

Here are some pointers to help you:

1. **Professionalism.** Do they have any accreditations or are they part of any marquee-specific memberships, such as MUTA?

2. **Service.** Do they offer a free site visit? Are they able to provide scaled computer-aided design (CAD) drawings? What emergency service do they offer on your wedding day; that is, do they provide a supervisor for your wedding day or do they have an emergency contact who would be available 24/7? Do they understand your vision? Are they prompt at replying to your enquiries? Do you feel confident they'll give you a stress-free experience?

3. **Quality.** Do they clean their marquee linings after each hire? Check their insurance documents, risk assessments, flame-retardancy certification, etc.

4. **Quotations.** Make sure you know what you're paying for. Does your marquee company give you choices for flooring, linings and furnishings? Do they include a damage-waiver fee? If you're comparing quotations, make sure you're comparing apples with apples, as there's a wide range of prices on the market.

5. **Customers.** Ask to see testimonials from previous customers. Check the company's social media thoroughly. Look at images of their previous work. Ask if they have an open day or a showcase where you could see examples of their marquees.

6. **Flexibility.** Have the conversation with your prospective marquee company about the possibility of making any changes to the marquee specification before your big day. For example, if during the week before your wedding it looks like heavy rain is forecast, would they be able to bolt on a porch or extend your marquee to create some extra undercover space? If the weather looks like it will be cold, would they allow you add a heater, etc.? Of course, there may be some things that just aren't practical, but asking the what-if questions at this stage will give you a good feel of how supportive they'll be to work with.

When you employ a wedding planner, all of the aforementioned due diligence is taken care of, which saves you an awful lot of leg work.

AN EXPERIENCED PLANNER WILL USE THEIR KNOWLEDGE AND BUSINESS RELATIONSHIPS TO RECOMMEND THE BEST COMPANIES FOR YOU TO WORK WITH, ALREADY KNOWING THE ANSWERS TO ALL THESE POINTS.

Doing a simple Google search won't answer these questions, so you can see just how much extra wedding admin this would be if you're searching independently.

Common Planning Mistakes

To make sure you enjoy your wedding planning and that everything is seamless, here are some common mistakes I frequently see couples make, so you can avoid making the same ones.

Poor budgeting

The most common mistake is not setting a budget. All too often, couples will begin planning the most expensive day of their lives with little consideration for the financials. Sadly, the usual end result is that the money doesn't stretch as far as it should, and couples have to make decisions on expenditure that could have been avoided, or they overspend and begin married life with massive credit card bills! My biggest tip is to do some research before you begin getting too carried away with booking suppliers. Approach your planning fully armed with research, priorities and a budget.

Badly planned timings

When it comes to your actual wedding day, think about a schedule. This will be so important for all the suppliers you've involved, and I'd certainly advise getting input on it from your photographer and caterer. If you've chosen the option of siting your marquee at a wedding venue, then do they have timing restrictions? The photographer will need to make sure they have enough time to capture all the shots you've requested, while considering the best light, backdrops and that all-important 'golden hour' (see the *Glossary* at the end of the book on page 141).

Include the travel time for your guests, especially if the wedding is over more than one site (for example, at a church then a marquee site), and include in this the time it takes to park multiple vehicles and for the walk your guests will be making in heels and posh clothes! Your caterer will need to know the times at which you wish to eat, cut the cake, have reception drinks, etc., so that the food doesn't spoil and so that your guests aren't subjected to a protracted wait for refreshments. In my book, you can never have too much detail on your timing schedule; even the most laid back of wedding days needs to have certain timing milestones to ensure everything happens in a calm and smooth way. Timings are discussed in the *Wedding-Day Timeline* chapter on page 84.

Not thinking about your guests

If I ask my couples what the most important thing about their wedding day is, the first thing they'll say is getting married, and the second thing will be that they get to have an amazing day with their guests, and that their guests will have a great time too. I've heard too many sad tales about guests not enjoying weddings so my adage is *"Happy guests, happy couple!"*

Common complaints from guests are them not being fed and watered at the right time(s), being given the wrong food or too little food/drink, not being comfortable (that is, being too hot or too cold, which is particularly a concern at outdoor summer weddings with no shade!), the speeches going on for too long, the music being too loud, being too squashed together during the meal, having too many group shots, and having a lack of information about the proceedings for the day.

Also, think about your smaller guests – there's nothing worse than grumpy, badly behaved children at weddings! Think about food and drink for them, their seating arrangements, and perhaps some activities to keep them entertained. Really think about designing your day with your guests in mind, so as to make sure that they leave your wedding with nothing but compliments and fabulous memories.

Photo booths are so popular and are a budget-friendly way to get some great photos.

HAVING NO CONTINGENCY PLAN

Top of the list here is the good old British weather! This is the one thing you have zero control over! My top advice is to plan for both rubbish and great weather, especially if you're having a summer wedding. I always say to my clients that if you plan for rain and then you get glorious sunshine, it's a bonus, but don't expect this and then be disappointed and upset if it rains!

So, *always* plan for the worst, whether this is having a stack of wellies ready and loads of umbrellas, the flexibility to have everyone inside your marquee, or reminding guests politely on the invitations you send out to be prepared for inclement weather; there are many options. Prepare a contingency plan for this. If it's wet and you are planning to be outside, *communicate* this to your whole wedding team, so that the venue, caterer, photographer, etc. can all be prepared.

MARQUEE MISTAKES

When it comes to planning a marquee wedding, there's a whole other set of things that can go wrong, which is why it's really important to make sure you curate a wedding team comprised of those who have experience of marquees.

> USING AN EXPERIENCED WEDDING PLANNER WHO KNOWS ABOUT MARQUEES CAN HELP YOU MASSIVELY AND SAVE YOU MONEY, BECAUSE WITH MARQUEES, MISTAKES CAN BE QUITE COSTLY.

Making the Most of Your Money

There's no getting away from the fact that weddings are expensive! It can seem like a never-ending stream of costs. Budgeting is by far the best way to set out on your planning journey in the right way, but you'll find there are inevitably things that pop up that you simply *must* have! Being sensible about your priorities and any ways you may be able to save money is an important method of controlling your costs. Another way to ensure you remain focused on spending in the right areas is to pinpoint the areas where adding a little extra budget can make a massive difference. Here are my **'plan like a pro' tips** on where you can *save* and where you should think about *splurging* your cash.

Flowers

Make a saving. Make your flowers multipurpose; by that, I mean you should move them around depending on where your guests are. Ask your florist to design arrangements for you that are transportable, just so you can get the maximum usage from them. For example, milk churns are great for framing ceremony locations or having at churches, and then moving them to become welcoming arrangements at your reception (if they fit with your style, of course!).

Pro tip: Use your bridal bouquet and bridesmaid's bouquets to dress part of your venue after the ceremony. They look great lined up on the top table or displayed in crystal vases round the cake.

Drinks

Make a saving. I often get asked by my clients about the etiquette of providing drinks for your guests. In my opinion, guests are completely happy (and often expect) to pay for their own drinks in the evening part of the wedding, so I'd suggest you have a pay bar. I'd also recommend researching the bar-hire company you wish to use to make sure they have either a small minimum spend for the evening or no minimum spend at all; this is just to make sure you don't get any nasty surprises in the form of an invoice after the wedding. This also gives you the flexibility later in the planning process to add in a portion of free drinks if you find you have some budget spare.

Pro tip: Check mobile phone coverage where you're siting the bar. If phone reception is patchy, then it could cause problems for card payments, as these work by linking up to the mobile phone networks. If this is the case, remind your guests to bring cash and let the bar team know.

Cool beers on a summer's afternoon!

STATIONERY

Make a saving. I've seen so many brides and grooms make their own stationery successfully, DIY style. But be warned, it can take time – especially if you're a perfectionist – so be prepared for sleepless nights! A few bits of beautifully crafted stationery are much better than a massive quantity that looks scruffy and isn't necessary, so budget wisely and consider where stationery will enhance your day and your guests' experiences. For example, is an elegant menu more use than a welcome sign? Do you need RSVP cards included with your invitations?

Pro tip: There are lots of companies that offer free wedding websites. These are specific websites that you set up with all your wedding information for your guests, and then you don't need to send out invitations or updates; your guests simply log on and check. They're a great cost-saving idea, and you can tie them in with your wedding design and colours. Just make sure you have an alternative if you're inviting anyone who doesn't have internet access (e.g. elderly relatives).

BRIDESMAIDS & GROOMSMEN

Make a saving. This might be slightly controversial, but it could save you hundreds of pounds! Firstly, think about the number of bridesmaids and groomsmen you'd like to have. If money is no object, then have as many as you want! Consider asking your bridesmaids if they could buy their dresses themselves. There was one wedding I planned a few years ago where the bride just asked her best ladies to buy their own choice of a knee-length, patterned dress and white shoes to wear – the brief was as loose as that. I have to say that they looked really pretty on the day, and by saving on the outfits, she was able to pay for them each to have their hair done professionally.

Also weigh up all the accessories they need; perhaps jewellery could double up as their thank you gift, you could ask them to wear shoes they already have in a certain colour, etc. Do they need their hair and make-up doing professionally or would they be happy to pay for this themselves?

Pro tip: If you're planning far enough in advance, make the most of the January sales and buy your bridesmaid dresses then; you could also consider selling them on eBay or similar after the wedding to recoup a bit of cash.

The bride and her best ladies.

Beautiful bouquets and table details.

Favours

Make a saving. There's a tradition of offering your guests wedding favours, but if you're feeling slightly unconventional, then skip the favours altogether. Otherwise, think about your favours doubling up as an extra snack or drink for your guests. I always think a little handmade cookie or home-made liqueur is a thoughtful, as well as useful, favour idea. At the end of the day, many favours get left behind by your guests, and they can clutter your beautiful place settings, so think carefully about whether you want to spend any budget on them at all.

Pro tip: If you do decide to have favours, consider creating them yourself to save some money and make them more personal. In my experience, the best favours are usually edible or drinkable! For example, you could make chocolate truffles / brownie bites or brew your own sloe gin.

Photographer

Splash the cash. So many people ask friends to take their wedding photos; trust me, this is one area you totally need a pro to take care of for you! By all means, have a friend as a second shooter, but not as your one and only record keeper of your special day. There are so many reasons for this, which have been well documented by numerous photographers, but it doesn't have to cost you the earth. If you only have £200 for a photographer and you're on a tight budget, then there are pros out there who will help. You certainly do get what you pay for, so if you can afford more, then I'd strongly advise you spend as much as you can on this one. Your wedding photos can't be replaced, so having a professional get the right composition, lighting and quality to your images will be worth it, I promise!

Of course, this is also true if you are hiring a videographer too.

Pro tip: If you feel you're tight on budget, only pay for a photographer to photograph the most important parts of the day for you (for example, just the ceremony or just the first dance).

CAKE

Make a saving. Cutting the wedding cake is often a significant point in the wedding day, marking the beginning of the dancing, and the time to really let your hair down and party! Consider ways of saving money on the cake if this is something that you're not overly bothered about. For example, think about portion size; although a large cake is showstopping, you'll be left with way too much cake to eat, which is just an expensive waste. Or you could contemplate incorporating your cake into a dessert bar for the evening; it could then be a smaller cake that's just for the ceremonial cutting, but you'd still be offering your guests a sweet selection of treats to pick from. How about a cheese cake made of different cheeses? This is perfect to then transform into a cheese buffet for your evening food. This is also one area where it can be cost-effective to call in a favour if you have a baker in the family.

Pro tip: Many supermarkets offer a budget-friendly wedding cake range. Consider this for your wedding cake, but then spend a bit of money on the decorating of it to make it look truly amazing.

VISUAL IMPACT

Splash the cash. You want your guests to remember your wedding day for all the right reasons, so make it memorable. Ponder how your guests will move through your marquee as your day progresses (you can see a floor-plan example in the *Marquee Floor Plans* chapter on page 81) and how your day will run.

I think every wedding should have one wow factor that is personal to the bride and groom. This could be arriving at your venue in a classic sports car or having the most amazing cake, but it's the one thing that really stands out, and makes it memorable and unique. It should be something that's impactful. It's no use investing budget in small details if you're strapped for cash; instead, think about creating one area that has the wow factor rather than diluting your budget on lots of different things.

Pro tip: In a marquee, the best use of your budget is to concentrate on creating a visual impact that's at your eye level or above; anything else is a waste.

FOOD

Splash the cash. Having hungry guests is something to avoid at all costs, and providing a good-quality dining experience (with respect to both the food and the service) will leave a lasting impression of how good your wedding day was for your guests. I'm not saying it needs to be Michelin-star quality – you still need to feed your guests based on what your budget constraints are.

Pro tip: There are also ways of using your budget in a creative way to make your food budget go further; for example, think about having a substantial canapé reception and foregoing a starter, or use your wedding cake as part of your dessert or evening food.

Firstly, to reduce stress, having a professional apply your make-up means that all you need to do is sit back, sip champagne and leave the worrying about how straight your eyeliner is to them! A make-up artist is adept at knowing how much time to take, so they will plan their timings to the minute, which will mean your getting-ready experience will be calm and under control.

Secondly, your make-up will be applied in the morning, before your wedding and will have to last all the way through to the small hours, while being picture-perfect throughout. This is a tall order, and a professional will know the tricks of the trade to ensure it all stays in place.

Thirdly, a professional will get the balance of your make-up right to ensure you look your best in any of the photographs. Photos can bleed you of colour, and you'll need to have your cosmetics applied in a way that allows your natural features to be defined clearly, but, more importantly, to still look like you (and not an orange Barbie version!). I recently saw some amazing wedding photos of a stunning bride, but her lipstick colour was so wrong for the lighting conditions that she actually looked like she didn't have any lips at all. This is something that can't be undone, and a pro will prevent this happening to you.

Pro tip: Have a trial run of your make-up! Make sure you get your ideal look nailed before your big day to help keep your bridal preparations as calm as possible.

SOURCING

Make a saving. When you receive your marquee quotation, the chances are that your marquee provider will include all the furniture, lighting, dance floor, toilets, power, etc. that you need for your wedding. While this is super helpful and means you're only dealing with one supplier for a whole host of things, it may not be the most budget-friendly tactic. If you feel able to, and have the time to do it, then search out other suppliers who can supply some of these elements. Compare prices, delivery and quality, as you can often make considerable savings by clever sourcing.

> **Pro tip:** Set up a spreadsheet to compare each of your supplier's quotes, then you'll get a clear picture for easy comparison. Score any aspects that are not quantifiable, such as the relevance of their experience, the speed of their response and how they made you feel, for example.

Section 2

THE PRACTICAL STUFF

Utilities

So you have a beautiful field, which is surrounded by unspoilt views of the countryside – that's brilliant, but there are some fundamentals that need putting into place in order to actually make your day work! Quite often, it's the case that there's literally nothing on your site, and I'm often asked by clients if it's possible to create a wedding venue on a site where there's exactly that. My answer is always yes, because you can bring to site whatever you need. I'm not saying that this is a cheap option. In fact, there's a common misconception that a marquee wedding is a budget option, but it isn't. You don't need to have a massive budget, but there are basics that need covering, costs that you wouldn't have and logistics you wouldn't need to worry about if you'd opted for a bricks-and-mortar venue.

Power

It's very unlikely that you'll have power on site if you're using a field. If you're hosting your wedding in your garden at home, then you may have some external power sockets that you can tap in to, but be warned – you need to be 100% certain that your electrics are going to be robust enough for this, as you'd have no backup if there was a failure.

There will be a cost for extra-long, weatherproof cabling if you do connect up to your domestic power supply, and the maximum distance you can run the electrics from the domestic supply to the marquee is 100m. However, my honest advice would be to get a professional, qualified electrician to double check that your domestic supply can handle all the equipment you'll be powering in your marquee, plus anything externally (for example, flood lights, portable toilets, food trucks, refrigerated vans, etc.).

The most common power source for a marquee is a generator, and these come in varying sizes depending on how much power you'll be drawing. The most common sizes of generator are 20kVA, 40kVA and 60kVA. It's most likely that you'd need a 40kVA generator for a wedding of about 100 guests, but don't cut it too fine; having a larger capacity one is always the better option, and it's usually for a relatively small cost increase. Generators can be noisy, but putting them behind the catering tent, the portable toilets or a screen of shrubbery (if your site has it) will help absorb the sound. Once your site is filled with chattering guests, the noise level of the generator will be barely audible.

They're towed onto site, usually by a small truck or 4x4, and quite often this is something your marquee company can arrange for you, as they can then set up what's called the 'distribution board', which all your 13A plug sockets will come from. You'll need to list everything that will be plugged into your generator, so that your electrician or marquee company can work out the size of generator you'll need, and also determine the number of 13A, 16A and 32A sockets your suppliers will need. Double check with each of your suppliers what power they'll need, the required position of the sockets and the equipment they'll be plugging in.

You'll need to make sure that your power supply is delivered at the same time as the marquee is being erected and that it's removed from the site afterwards, before your marquee is struck, so that the marquee company can hook up the lighting to the power and then do the same in reverse. In addition, double check the backup plan for your generator; if it fails, is there a call-out number you can ring and will someone come out? Always using a reliable, reputable company is imperative when it comes to your power. Also, having a local contractor for the generator will lower your delivery costs, and it'll make it much easier to coordinate delivery, collection and any possible call-outs.

Check if there are any costs associated with additional cables; these may be an extra charge on top of the hire fee for your generator. Find out how you'll be charged for fuel; some generator companies will charge you after your event for the fuel you used, and others may include one full tank as part of the hire charge. It's worthwhile having someone keep an eye on the fuel consumption, and if necessary, make sure you have a can of diesel at the ready – stored safely – for emergency top-ups. The likelihood is that you'll use the generator during the setting up of your marquee and to test equipment the day before your wedding, so always check on the morning of the wedding that you have plenty of fuel to see you through the day, as the generator will be running pretty much continuously from that point on.

You may want to consider hiring two generators that work in tandem, so that if one fails – and it can happen – the other one will kick into action, giving you seamless power. This is really a case of playing the what-if game, but consider what could happen if, for example, there was no power and the generator company couldn't get anyone to you for two hours. It's obviously an additional cost, but it's certainly something to seriously consider.

Generators are very expensive to replace, and fairly easy to steal from a field, so it could be that you need to think about putting some overnight security in place to keep your site safe. This could even be as simple as having some friends camp inside your marquee overnight.

Water

Getting water to your site can be achieved in a number of different ways. The simplest way is to use an existing external water tap, as long as it's potable water. Catering teams would then either fill larger vessels for their use or run a hygienically prepared water pipe from the outside tap to the catering tent. Other options could be to hire a water supply; I've used office-water-supply companies for this in the past, which deliver large 15L water bottles to the site, and will remove the empty and unused bottles afterwards. Other options (depending on your number of guests) could be to purchase lots of water from a cash-and-carry or supermarket. Your catering team will need some water for washing-up, but the largest drain on your supply will be for boiling water for cooking, teas and coffees, and drinking water. Remember, drinking water won't just be required to accompany your wedding breakfast; keeping your guests hydrated throughout the whole wedding is really important.

Toilets

Even if you're hosting your wedding at home, I'd suggest hiring portable toilets. You may wish to keep your home locked up, your facilities may not withstand excessive use on the day, and would you have enough toilets to cater for your number of guests? Portable toilets come in many guises, and all they need is a 13A socket. They get emptied off site, and have separate ladies and gents.

One important question to ask here is do you have disabled guests or many children attending? Most portable toilet blocks have steps leading up to them, so if you do need disabled access or a baby-changing facility, then consider hiring a toilet with disabled access as well.

There are lots of options to choose from, varying in size and luxury, so do some research and speak to your marquee company for recommendations too. When you're picking your toilet supplier, you'll see them referred to as 2+1, 3+1, etc. These numbers refer to the sizes of the toilets: a 2+1 means that in the men's side there are two urinals and one cubicle, and then two cubicles in the ladies' side as well.

Toilet blocks are usually brought onto the site on the back of a trailer towed by a 4x4, so you'll need to consider how much swinging space there is for manoeuvring them into position. They usually have a light on the outside, but you may need to add some extra lighting to help guests navigate their way safely to find them, and some signage to show where they are if they're tucked away.

I often recommend that my clients add their own little touches to the toilets as well, just to personalise them and make them feel more special. This could simply be a beautiful-smelling reed diffuser; a lovely, scented soap with matching hand cream; a posy of fresh flowers; or a mini vanity kit.

*Some suggestions for your toilet vanity kit:**

PORTABLE TOILET VANITY KIT

CHECKLIST

What to include in your guest toilets:

- ☐ Tissues
- ☐ Paracetemol
- ☐ Plasters
- ☐ Sun Lotion and Aftersun
- ☐ Insect Bite Cream
- ☐ Insect Repellent
- ☐ Antacid
- ☐ Deodorant Spray
- ☐ Make-up Wipes
- ☐ Hair Grips
- ☐ Hair Spray
- ☐ Breath Mints
- ☐ Antibacterial Hand Gel
- ☐ Antiseptic Cream / Spray
- ☐ Cooling Spray

**Included in your checklist pack*

Catering

If you're planning on feeding your guests during your wedding day, then you'll need a field kitchen or catering tent in which your catering team can set up and operate for the day. Each team will have their own specific requirements, so I'd highly recommend you double check with them what they'll need (and it may even depend on your exact menu, so don't panic if the details need tweaking as you get further down the line with your planning).

Very generally speaking, a catering tent of around 6m x 6m is usually adequate for about 80–100 guests. This will need carpet flooring (and, ideally, for the ground to be as flat as possible), lighting and direct access into the main marquee, so the team can serve the meals as quickly and efficiently as possible. It's also worth noting that, in most cases, the catering tent will also house what's known as the 'distribution board', which is for all your electrics.

It's also important to make sure there's access at the back of the catering tent that the team can drive a vehicle up to for unloading/loading and clearing away discreetly, and I'd advise providing some external lighting at the back of the catering tent so they can see clearly what they're doing at the end of the night.

Depending on the orientation and location of your catering tent in relation to your main marquee, you may need to consider including a baffle screen at the entrance. A baffle screen is a staggered entrance that prevents guests from seeing directly into the kitchen area.

EQUIPMENT

In terms of equipment, the catering tent will need to have plenty of tables – ideally, metal ones from a hygiene perspective, but if not, then wooden trestle tables. They'll also need at least one large water boiler, an oven (gas or convection will be down to the preference of your chef) and probably a hot cupboard, as a minimum.

Another piece of equipment they'll need is some sort of fridge. Many caterers will bring their own refrigerated van, but if they don't have one, then they'll most likely ask you to hire a large one.

The other items required will depend on your menu, and they'll be things such as a deep fat fryer or a freezer; for any other small appliances needed (for example, whisks), your caterer will bring their own. Sometimes, you'll need to provide dustbins, tea towels, aprons, trays, bar-service equipment, etc. Basically, you're equipping a kitchen that will be used to cook a three-course meal, so every single item will need to be brought on site, so just get clarity on exactly what your catering team will bring with them, and what you're responsible for sourcing, ordering and paying for.

Waste

The subject of waste disposal is often a topic that gets overlooked. You'll need to read the fine print on your site agreement to make sure you completely cover what is contracted in terms of removing rubbish from the marquee site. In my experience, the simplest option by far is to hire a small skip that any waste can be put into. You may, however, be lucky and have a catering company who will take most of the food rubbish, and if you're hiring a bar company, then empty bottles and bar debris is their responsibility. Again, read the small print in your terms and conditions or contracts, so you are 100% sure, because it could be a nasty shock the morning after your wedding! Also make certain that if any food is left on site overnight, it's securely tied up in bin bags or properly stored in sealed containers, and the whole marquee is secured properly overnight to prevent any unwanted visitors ransacking the leftovers (and by that I mean foxes, deer, rats, etc.)!

Washing-up

One of the questions a lot of my clients always ask me is what to do about the washing-up. When you hire glasses, cutlery and crockery, most of these hire companies will deliver everything to your site clean and ready to use, then they'll remove everything dirty, so the only items that are likely to be washed up on site are the cooking pots and pans belonging to the catering team. This is particularly important to remember when it comes to your glassware, because you'll need to order enough for your whole event, as washing-up midway through isn't going to be very practical. This is even more complex to calculate when you're providing the drinks for your whole wedding and you don't want to serve them in disposable plastic cups. It's possible to hire glass-washers, but this doesn't make practical sense when you compare the cost of ordering extra glasses to the hire cost and additional tasks of linking up the glass-washer to running water and power.

One important point to note is that you must ensure your catering team are aware of any restrictions on the disposal of dirty liquids on site; for example, some marquee sites do not permit you to pour away dirty washing-up water or drinks remnants, as it can cause fatty deposits on the ground and attract rats, foxes and insects. So, you'll need to make certain that there's an agreed safe space for the disposal of waste water.

Bar Hire and TENs

First of all, let me explain what a TEN is: it stands for temporary event notice, and you apply for these through your local council. They usually cost around £21 (at the time of writing), and they allow you to hold a licensable event in an unlicensed venue in England or Wales. Licensable activities are the sale of alcohol, providing entertainment or offering late-night refreshments.

For a pay bar, you'll definitely need to have a TEN. Your bar-hire company can take care of this for you, or they may have their own personal licence. If you're having your wedding at an established venue, then the likelihood is that you won't need to worry about this, but if you're hosting at home or at an unlicensed venue, then you'll need to contact your local council and check their requirements.

For a TEN, you'll need to decide on a time at which you'll finish serving alcohol. You may also need to have your TEN cover your evening music, but this will depend on your location.

Making it Legal

As a reminder, this book is intended to help you with your planning, and it's up to you to make sure all of this is in place. Although I have offered some advice in this section, I am not a lawyer, so you need to make sure you have done your due diligence regarding what licences are needed before obtaining the ones legally necessary. In addition, legislation does change, and things may have changed between the time of writing and when you are reading this book.

THE FINANCES

There are lots of ways to supply your guests with drinks, but it'll predominantly depend on your budget. In order of most expensive to least expensive, here are the options you have (assuming you don't have a venue with its own restrictions):

» **If money is no object**, then it is a lovely treat to provide your guests with drinks throughout the day and evening. You don't necessarily need to have a fully stocked bar, though; you could limit it to a couple of spirits; red, white and prosecco wine; a couple of lagers and ales; and a few soft drinks too (e.g. water, orange juice, lemonade, and regular and diet cola).

» Using a **sale-or-return** option from one of the wine merchants is another way to make your budget go slightly further and to ensure you don't have to worry about running out!

» **To save a bit of money**, you could look at providing reception drinks and wine for your wedding breakfast, and then switch to a pay bar for your guests in the evening. A variation on this is to then put a tab behind the bar for a limited amount, so that your guests in the evening get at least some drinks before they have to pay.

» **Use a voucher system.** Each guest is provided with a set number of vouchers, each of which can be exchanged for a drink that you'll have prepaid for. After their vouchers have been used, your guests will have to pay for their drinks themselves.

» Have an **honesty-style bar** where you supply the drink, but your guests pay a voluntary amount for each drink, so you can recoup a little of the outlay. This would still be viewed as 'selling' alcohol, so you'd still need a TEN.

» **Have a pay bar for the whole event.** This is perhaps not the most popular option for your guests, and you may get some negative responses, so you should definitely forewarn your guests if this is your plan.

A TYPICAL WEDDING-DAY DRINKS MENU

I think it's just as important to consider your choice of beverages as it is to plan your food menu. Both should complement each other, and reflect your personalities, the style of your wedding and the season.

When your guests arrive after your ceremony, it's nice to greet everyone with a welcome drink. This could be anything from Pimm's to champagne. These drinks are usually pre-poured and passed around on trays, for guests to take one glass easily from a passing waiter. I'd recommend you pick something that appeals to the masses and is easy to serve for this part of your day. Drinks such as a gin and tonic or a cocktail don't tend to be as good when they're mixed en masse, and they can be quite time consuming to prepare, so you'd need to review your drinks team's staffing levels to deliver these sorts of drinks more carefully.

You must think about the presentation as well, so pick some glassware that reflects your style or is appropriate to the drink, and garnish them so they look beautiful.

Don't forget a soft drink option for your reception. I always think it's nice to offer something that can be served in the same style of glass as the alcoholic version; for example, elderflower cordial would be a complementary soft option to sit alongside a glass of fizz.

Bottles of chilled lager are usually popular with the chaps.

Get creative with your bar decor.

Personalise your bar with your favourite tipples.

Also make sure there's lots of plain water available. This could be in bottles or from a large self-service Kilner jar.

For your wedding breakfast, wine is the natural choice. You'll typically need to offer both a red and a white option as a minimum. These can be served in a variety of ways: your waiting team could pour them on demand, you could have the bottles left open on the table for guests to help themselves to, or you could use a combination of both (for example, the first glass can be poured by the waiting team then the guests can serve themselves after that). Ask your waiting team to replenish the bottles on demand to keep your tables less cluttered. You should also ensure your white wine is chilled and your red wine bottles have been opened to allow the wine time to breathe. Whether you'll need wine chillers on each table will depend on the timings and staffing levels of your day; if you can avoid the extra cost and the space they take up on the table, then I would.

When it comes to speeches, it will again be personal preference whether you wish to toast with something fizzy or with whatever your guests are drinking at the time. If you're serving fizz, then make sure you have enough clean glasses for each guest, and I'd recommend having your waiting team pass each guest a prefilled glass at the allotted time. Also, make sure you allow enough time in your schedule to pour and serve this, as it can take a good 20 minutes to fill 100 champagne flutes.

Once the wedding breakfast is over, then drinks service will switch to your bar, whether this is done by a separate company or your catering team is running it for you.

You might want some bubbles to go with the speeches.

What is corkage?

If you choose the option of having a marquee at a wedding venue, then corkage is something you need to be aware of. However, if you choose to have a marquee in a field, then you don't need to worry about this.

'Corkage' is a fee per bottle consumed (usually different fees for fizz, wine and spirits) that the venue will charge you for the consumption on their premises of alcohol that they haven't supplied. This does give you the freedom to select the exact drinks you wish to serve; however, the fee per bottle is sometimes as much as the cost of the house wine the venue would supply anyway, so you're unlikely to make a saving. If corkage is being charged, then you must make certain that you are aware of and understand all the terms for this. I'd suggest you ask about the following: when they count the bottles, and who is responsible for that; whether they supply glassware, chilling facilities and serving equipment; when they send the invoice for this cost; what happens with half-drunk bottles; whether the venue provides you with any serving staff for your drinks; and who's responsibility the empty bottles are.

Dry-bar hire

Dry-bar hire is where you hire the physical bar and then you provide everything else yourself. You can pick the style that works best with your wedding, whether it's a rustic-style pallet bar or a more elegant, mirrored, circular one. It's great to be able to tie this in with your styling, to create a cohesive visual look across your marquee. For your dry bar, you'll need to think about everything from bottle openers to the disposal of the empties, as it'll be your responsibility. This type of bar doesn't come with staffing or any equipment; you literally hire the structure of it.

Depending on how you want to run it, you could do one of the following:

- Have a free-for-all so guests just help themselves
- Have your catering team run the bar for you – keeping on top of portion sizes, dirties and empties can be worth the money; or
- Have a team of bar specialists come and run the service, bringing all their own equipment and just using your structure.

*Here's a checklist of the equipment you'll need to run your bar:**

DIY BAR

CHECKLIST

What you need to equip your dry-hire bar:

- ☐ Glassware – think about different styles for the different drinks you are offering
- ☐ Bottle openers and corkscrews
- ☐ Ice, ice buckets and tongs
- ☐ Garnishes, e.g. lemons, limes, cherries and straws
- ☐ Chilling facilities, e.g. trailer, fridge, and / or large ice buckets
- ☐ Multiple rubbish bins – so you can separate recycling from general waste
- ☐ Knife and chopping board for prepping garnishes –pre-slice if you can, though
- ☐ Mixers and water
- ☐ Do you need pumps / stills for beers, lagers or ales? Or are you serving bottles only?
- ☐ Signage with your drinks selection and prices
- ☐ Cloths / tea towels for spillages
- ☐ Mixers, shakers and stirrers if you are serving cocktails
- ☐ Spirit measures
- ☐ Lighting
- ☐ Dustpan and brush for breakages

**Included in your checklist pack*

Drink quantities

One factor you must consider when providing a dry bar yourselves is how much drink (alcohol and soft drinks) you may need. The following gives a very rough rule of thumb to use as a gauge, but other factors that may be in play include the age of your guests, the ratio of men to women among your guests, and the weather, for example.

- **Reception drinks.** The rule of thumb here is one drink per guest every half an hour. If you're serving fizz, then you'll typically get eight flutes filled per bottle.
- **Wedding breakfast drinks.** It would be usual to offer wine to accompany your wedding breakfast, and I'd allow half a bottle of wine per guest. For a standard bottle of wine, you'll be able to pour six glasses of wine. If your menu is more than three courses, for example, a tasting menu, then this would increase.
- **Speech/toast drinks.** If you're serving fizz for the toasts during your speeches, then the easiest way to calculate this is simply one glass per person (excluding children).
- **Evening drinks.** This is the hardest part to calculate (and is often why a lot of couples opt for a pay bar in the evening, so they don't need to worry about running out of alcohol!). Again, a rule of thumb would be one drink per guest every half an hour.

Marquee Floor Plans

I think one of the most challenging parts of planning a marquee wedding is that you never get to see, or experience, the finished product until your wedding day. This can be really difficult if you're a control freak or find it challenging to visualise things. Marquee companies hold open days, and some may let you visit a marquee they've erected for another client. Of course, this would only be the structure itself; it wouldn't be fully laid out and decorated to your exact specifications.

A good-quality marquee provider will supply you with what's known as a CAD drawing of your layout; this is a computer-generated drawing, which will be to scale. It should also show how your main furniture elements will fit into the space (for example, the tables and chairs, dance floor and bar). It's incredibly useful to get this produced before you pay your marquee deposit, so you can get a feel of how your ideal layout will work.

The marquee drawings are just of the marquee itself and don't usually include the whole site (elements such as the generator, toilet block, parking and access points are excluded), so if you have any doubts about this, then I'd recommend sketching a site map. This can be really useful to share with any suppliers, so you'll have a definitive plan to show them of how your whole day will flow.

Creating your own floor plan will allow you to see if everything fits (assuming you can create it to scale), and it'll also help you to make sure that you have enough space for your service team to access your guests' tables, and that there's a 'flow' through your marquee. It's a visual aide you can quickly share with the suppliers involved.

I also think it lets you start to see your day through your guest's eyes, so you can get a handle on things such as these: what the first thing they see as they enter your marquee will be, how your day will progress through your marquee, what will draw your guests' attention and how you can use the space in the best possible way.

Once you have your floor plan drafted, it's a great starting point to really finesse your day and create your wedding design.

One of the key parts of the service I offer is working on your bespoke floor plan and marquee layout to make sure that logistically, it works smoothly and, aesthetically, it looks cohesive and beautiful. In your checklist pack, you'll find a quick list of all the elements you'll need to consider including on your plan. *This floor plan has been created in specialised software by Marquee Tech.*

*Here's your marquee floor-plan checklist:**

MARQUEE FLOOR-PLAN

CHECKLIST

What you may need to include:

- [ ] Entrance and entrance space
- [ ] Dancefloor
- [ ] Band floor space / staging
- [ ] Wedding breakfast tables
- [ ] Top table
- [ ] Cake table
- [ ] Catering kitchen
- [ ] Casual seating
- [ ] Tea and coffee station
- [ ] Gift table
- [ ] Bar
- [ ] Service space for reception drinks, e.g. trestle table
- [ ] Any other entertainment, e.g. photo booth, glitter bar or chocolate fountain
- [ ] Freestanding décor, e.g. lighting, floral arrangements and trees
- [ ] Table for escort cards or space for a table plan
- [ ] Space for a welcome sign
- [ ] Any structural elements, e.g. king poles

**Included in your checklist pack*

Wedding-Day Timeline

Having a comprehensive wedding-day timeline is imperative to having a smooth-flowing, stress-free day. A lot of couples will come to me and say they want a relaxed, chilled day, but believe me, in order to achieve this you have to plan and have a timeline that's well thought through. A lot of your suppliers will ask for rough timings when you book their services or are requesting quotations, so some of your timings will be confirmed fairly early on in your planning, but you'll need to refine them as your planning becomes more detailed and your wedding-day plans are finalised.

I think there are three versions of your wedding-day timeline that you need to put together when you're having a marquee wedding. It may sound like overkill, but bear with me, and I'll explain the differences and why each is important in its own right.

Schedule One: The Guest Schedule

The first one is a guest-friendly version. This can be sent out with your invitations and put on your wedding website, then this can be communicated on the day via an 'order of the day' signage board or printed as part of your orders of service, for example. This timeline will inform your guests about the key events during the day that they need to know about. Food and drink are obviously a critical part of your day, so pop on this timeline what time the reception drinks will be, when your wedding breakfast will be served, what time the bar opens and when the evening food will be served.

Other times that your guests will need to be aware of are those for the key moments in your day, such as the start of your ceremony, group photos, speeches, cutting the cake, your first dance and the end time. Your guests will want to make sure they're at the right spot for each of these events, and that they haven't disappeared for a toilet break or anything at a critical moment!

SCHEDULE TWO: THE DETAILED SCHEDULE

The second timeline will be seriously detailed and will take you from the moment you're awake on your wedding day through to the very end of the day. When you first sit down to compose this, you won't know what time you need to get up on your wedding day, so the easiest way to work out this schedule is to begin with the timings that are immovable. It's highly likely that the most immovable time will be your ceremony, so put that down first and work backwards. If you have a registrar holding your legal ceremony, then they will need to complete separate interviews (of roughly 15 minutes each) with both you and your future spouse, so time will need to be put into the schedule for these; the bride arriving late to a registrar-led ceremony is not the done thing!

Working backwards from your ceremony time, determine your travel time to the ceremony (if you're using a vintage vehicle, these don't travel as fast as modern cars, so you may need to allow a little extra time to be on the safe side). Ask your transport provider to do a dry run before your wedding day so they know the route, whether there are any roadworks/delays and the exact timings. Make sure you leave enough time between when you're ready and when you need to leave for your ceremony to take some last-minute deep breaths and photos; remember, you won't get this day again, so make sure you allow your photographer enough time to document everything you want them to.

> YOUR HAIRDRESSER AND MAKE-UP ARTIST WILL EACH ALLOCATE A CERTAIN AMOUNT OF TIME FOR EACH PERSON WHO NEEDS THEIR SERVICES, SO WORK BACKWARDS FROM WHEN YOU WANT TO BE READY. IT MAY BE THAT, FOR THE NUMBER OF PEOPLE YOU HAVE INCLUDED, THEY'LL NEED TO RECRUIT EXTRA PEOPLE TO MAKE SURE EVERYONE IS BEAUTIFIED IN GOOD TIME.

Also, make sure you allow enough time to get into your dress, especially if it has lots of buttons or lacing that need extra care. If your photographer is going to take some getting-ready shots, then double check with your florist that your bridal flowers will have been delivered in enough time for this to happen. The same applies if your groom is getting ready at an

Don't rush getting ready; enjoy it and don't get flustered!

Plan your entrance carefully – it will be a photo opportunity.

Use your ceremony time as the kingpin for your timeline.

alternative location – is he going to have his buttonhole delivered by the florist? Also, will your photographer have enough time, taking into account the travel time required, to shoot at both locations? It may be that if this is something you both definitely want to incorporate into your wedding day, you may need to hire a second shooter; this is completely possible, so check your rough timeline with your photographer in plenty of time ahead of your wedding so that arrangements can be made if required.

Ideally, on the morning of your wedding, you don't want to be worrying about putting the finishing touches in your marquee personally, as this can be a major time suck, put out all of your timings and make you rush your getting-ready time, which is just too stressful.

While you're getting ready, make sure you drink plenty of water and eat regular snacks; you'll probably be feeling nervous and excited, but force yourself to do this, as fainting during your ceremony is definitely not a good idea!

Also, in your timings for the things happening before your ceremony, you should include the movements of the other suppliers arriving at the marquee (for example, the catering team, bar company, possibly a DJ or band who will need to set up, anyone doing the final finishing touches to the marquee and the person delivering your cake). It's really important to include as much detail as you can, so that any suppliers involved in the organisation – such as an on-the-day coordinator or your event manager – know who'll be on site doing what and when. While you're getting ready, you don't really want to be taking any calls querying the set-up details, so delegate this to someone or employ a wedding planner specifically to manage all of this for you.

Assuming your ceremony has run to time, you can then move on to the next part of your celebration.

YOUR WEDDING-DAY TIMELINE SHOULD BE A WORKING DOCUMENT THAT ALL YOUR WEDDING SUPPLIERS ARE AWARE OF AND BUY INTO. ASK EACH OF THEM FOR THEIR INPUT, THEN MAKE ANY AMENDMENTS AND RECONFIRM WITH THE SUPPLIERS ANY CHANGES THAT MAY AFFECT THEM.

SCHEDULE THREE: THE OVERVIEW SCHEDULE

In addition to your wedding-day timeline, I'd definitely recommend you create a schedule for the week before your wedding and for a few days afterwards. This schedule should cover supplier movements on site (for example, when the marquee company is going to arrive and erect it, when the toilets will be delivered, which day your florist will be on site to decorate the marquee, and whether your catering team will arrive the day before to do any prep work). The part for after your wedding – which will schedule in who will be on site when to remove their equipment, hire items, etc. – is also really helpful, especially if you and your new husband/wife have left for a honeymoon, as you can leave this detail in the capable hands of someone else to coordinate on your behalf.

The benefit of producing a schedule this way is that you get your suppliers to commit to the exact times and days when they'll be delivering, and you'll have visibility of the whole set-up, so you can see if there are any clashes or if any of the timings are not in the correct sequence (there's no point having the table and linens delivered before the marquee is erected, for example).

How To Make Your Day Run Smoothly

Putting some time aside to make sure you have plans in place to guarantee that your wedding day actually runs perfectly is so important. Having spent so much time pulling together an amazing wedding day, you'll want it to be seamless and smooth-running. The key is in your preparations. Don't leave everything to the last minute and do tap into the expertise of your suppliers to make certain nothing is forgotten.

If your marquee site is close to any neighbouring properties, out of courtesy, I'd highly recommend you mention that you're hosting your wedding, and they may hear an increase in noise, traffic, etc. Always approach this sympathetically; the last thing you want are upset neighbours who then make a complaint to the police. Be clear with timings and what sort of disruption they may expect; perhaps offer a bottle of wine as a thank you to smooth the waters if you think it could be a problem. Always reassure the neighbours with the plans you're putting in place to ensure a well-managed wedding. By using clear signage and strategic lighting, you can prevent any trespassing on neighbouring land and make sure guests park where they should. If you're having your wedding at home and you get on well with your neighbours, then why not invite them along to the wedding or the evening? They're less likely to be concerned if they're enjoying the party too!

Planning your timelines meticulously and coordinating with your suppliers to make sure your timings will actually work is going to be pivotal to having a smooth-running wedding. Contingency planning and delegating key tasks will also remove a lot of the stress and worry from you and your new spouse, so you can relax and enjoy your day.

Another thing that is easy to organise in advance and that you'll find a great help on the day is an emergency kit. My emergency kit is extensive and contains all manner of things, as it's my job to be prepared for your special day. The following is an example one (which is also in your checklist pack) of what you may wish to include in your emergency kit. I'd recommend collecting these together in a big box or holdall for easy access for anyone involved in your marquee preparations. For easy access in case of emergencies, store it in the corner of the marquee, behind the lining, in the catering tent or under a table.

*Here's your emergency kit checklist:**

EMERGENCY KIT

CHECKLIST

Having these on standby will help your day run smoothly:

- ☐ Scissors
- ☐ Selection of pens
- ☐ Phone charger
- ☐ Lighters
- ☐ Blu Tack / White Tack / glue dots
- ☐ Pins (drawing, safety and hair)
- ☐ Emergency sewing kit
- ☐ Blank place cards
- ☐ Spare candles and batteries
- ☐ Supplier contact sheet (including emergency numbers)
- ☐ Spare timing schedule
- ☐ Tapes (Sellotape, masking, duct and double-sided)
- ☐ Spare ribbon, twine, string, etc.
- ☐ Baby wipes
- ☐ Tissues and cotton buds
- ☐ Ant and fly spray
- ☐ Tape measure and ruler
- ☐ Spare extension cable
- ☐ Floral wire
- ☐ Cable ties
- ☐ Bulldog clips
- ☐ Duster cloth and polish
- ☐ Dustpan and brush
- ☐ Tea towel
- ☐ Envelopes
- ☐ Torch
- ☐ Pegs
- ☐ White chalk

**Included in your checklist pack*

Should I Use a Wedding Planner?

The short answer is yes, but let me explain why this is a good idea and how it can help you. It's worth mentioning that not all wedding planners work the same way or offer the same services, so doing your due diligence is super important. Most will offer a free initial conversation, so do take advantage of that to speak to them about your ideas, and find out more about them and how they can help you.

If you're both happy and prepared to devote to your wedding the 300-odd hours needed to plan it, then maybe having the support of a wedding planner during the planning phase may not be the best use of your budget. However, it's worth noting that a wedding planner is a good investment during the planning phase, as they can help ensure that you keep to your budget, help you create your overall design, and support you with the logistical elements specific to a marquee – assuming you choose a planner who has experience of marquees.

Do note that not all planners offer the same services. A full wedding-planning service will cover pretty much everything involved in your wedding, whereas an on-the-day service will kick in shortly before your wedding to focus only on delivering your day. Someone who only provides on-the-day services may call themselves a wedding coordinator, and will have a slightly different skill set to a wedding planner, so just make sure you do your research.

Having a wedding planner whose service will help you to run the actual day is definitely something to consider, particularly with a marquee wedding. Having a planner will relieve you of the pressure on the day caused by worrying whether everything will happen as you wish it to. With this style of wedding, especially if you're on private land, there will be no kingpin working to ensure that everything happens as it should. The catering team are skilled at making sure your food is perfect and your guests are looked after, but what about checking the toilets, or dealing with any marquee or guest emergencies? Who will make sure any finishing touches are carried out as per your plans? An on-the-day wedding coordinator will make sure that you can relax and enjoy your special day, safe in the knowledge that someone else is worrying about your band getting fed or the public address (PA) system working!

IF YOU'RE LOOKING FOR SOMEONE TO TAKE THIS STRAIN, THEN GET IN TOUCH; ALL MY DETAILS ARE ON PAGE 139/140.

Contingency Planning

I know this isn't the most glamorous element of planning your wedding, but it can honestly make the difference between a fantastic day and a nightmare one! With some foresight and planning, you can ensure everything runs smoothly, your guests enjoy themselves and you limit your stress!

What if it's wet?

This is the most typical concern of couples having a marquee wedding, and to be honest, it's only something you need to really worry about when you're planning on being outside for a long period of time; for example, for group photos, reception drinks or even your ceremony (if you're planning an outside one). Guests moving between locations – to toilets, car parks, etc. – isn't such an issue, and the most simple and cost-effective option for that is to have a stash of umbrellas or ponchos to hand that people can borrow.

However, for prolonged periods of time outside, then you need consider having contingency plans. You could look at moving the location – for example, using the inside of your marquee for group shots, the ceremony or reception drinks – or you could look at adding a covered space outside, such as a gazebo or second marquee. If you're looking to use your inside space in this situation, then make certain you have a big enough empty area and that if any pieces of furniture need moving to make space, your wedding team know to move them and then put them back when they're required. With a marquee, this isn't always an easy option in itself, as there's unlikely to be any storage for tables and chairs, and your catering team and florist will most likely have already laid the tables and prepared them for your wedding breakfast. However, if needs must, then put a plan in place for this scenario.

Make sure you get advice on your contingency plan from your marquee company, catering team, photographer, videographer and any other suppliers (for example, the celebrant, wedding planner or master of ceremonies) that will be involved in the actual running of your day. And when you have your backup plans confirmed, communicate them effectively and ensure everyone knows exactly who is going to be the key person who will initiate activating the contingency plan.

SOME THINGS THAT MAY BE ADVISABLE TO INCLUDE IN YOUR WET-WEATHER PLAN ARE HAVING COVERED WALKWAYS; DOUBLE-GLAZED GABLE ENDS; WALLS OR DOORWAYS FOR ADDED INSULATION; RAISED FLOORING UNDER THE MARQUEE THAT WILL LIFT THE FLOOR OFF THE GROUND IN CASE IT BECOMES TOO FLOODED AND AN ADJOINING TOILET BLOCK WITH A MARQUEE EXTENSION.

If the weather is wet, there's also the likelihood that your guests will get cold, so I'd highly recommend having a backup plan for heating. Watch the weather in the month leading up to your big day. Having the BBC weather app on your phone is great for this, but there are other more accurate meteorological apps, such as Dark Skies, Weather Radar and Weather Underground, among others. If your wedding day is looking like it will be showery, it may be worth considering simply adjusting your timings slightly to avoid any forecast downpours.

I know that wet weather is something every bride dreads, but it really doesn't need to be the case; you'll be surrounded by friends and family who are all there to enjoy your day, and that's exactly what they'll do! Oh, and the photos? Well, rain can be stunning!

Turn rain into something amazing!

What if it's too hot?

You wouldn't instantly think this could be a problem, but there are a number of extra things you need to consider if your wedding is in the middle of a heatwave.

Similarly to if you have wet weather, one of your chief concerns when there is hot weather will be your guests:

- **Shade**. If you're hoping to have a substantial amount of your day outside during the hottest part of the day, then consider whether you need to add some extra shade with a couple of gazebos, for example. You may also need to provide some shade for any musicians who will be playing outside as well.
- **Hydration.** Being dehydrated is one of the worst things your guests could suffer from on a wedding day; with the consumption of alcohol and the exposure to lots of sun while wearing a suit, it's a bad combination. Ensuring you have plenty of drinking water readily available for your guests is imperative. You can get really creative with this: you could personalise little water bottles; you could stack a wheelbarrow with lots of bottles and ice; you could have a hydration station that's prettily decorated with paper cups, straws and Kilner jars of water or cordial; or you could install a water fountain, for example.
- **Food.** Your catering team will be completely on top of all the food safety regulations relating to the food they're supplying, but consider anything you're giving your guests that isn't provided by them (for example, your cake or any evening food). If you have a cake covered in cream or buttercream that's on display in your marquee from before your guests arrive up until when it's served in the evening, you may need to put provisions in place for storing it. Speak to your cake designer and find out how long it could be left unrefrigerated, and try to find a spot inside the marquee that isn't in direct sunlight. In the heat, your marquee will become like a greenhouse!

I'm frequently asked about installing air conditioning in a marquee, in the event that the weather is unbearably hot. In my experience, this is only going to have a limited impact on the temperature because of the nature of a marquee's construction. It can be very costly to install and is not easily available. In my opinion, you may be better considering adjusting the timings of your day and lifting the sides of your marquee to create a through-breeze.

Suppliers

When you're in the planning phase with your suppliers, do ask them what they will be putting in place to ensure there will be no hiccups with the service they're providing. This could be anything from having backup vegetarian meals or spare cutlery to checking what your photographer would do if they got ill or lost your files. Read their contracts to find out what backups they have in place.

> WORK WITH YOUR SUPPLIERS TO COVER THE MAIN EVENTUALITIES THAT WORRY YOU, SO YOU CAN CREATE SOME WORST-CASE SCENARIOS AND SOLUTIONS YOU'D FEEL COMFORTABLE WITH.

On the Day

As I mentioned before, being meticulous in your planning and preparation can really pay dividends when it comes to ensuring you have the best day ever.

Here are some of my recommendations for the things that you should have that will make sure your day goes smoothly:

- Your timelines.
- A table plan with guests' dietary requirements.
- Spare copies of your ceremony readings.
- Your emergency kit on standby.
- A copy of the on-the-day supplier contact details in case of an emergency.
- A designated person who can kick contingency plans into action and be an emergency contact point for any staff on the day, so you don't get pestered.
- Copious lists of what needs to be done and by whom! You can never have too many.
- Your confirmed contingency plans.

SETTING UP ON THE DAY

I expect you'll be planning to spend most of the day before your wedding setting up your marquee. Bearing in mind that your catering team, florist and possibly even your marquee company may need access to complete their preparations, you'll need to create a schedule of who will be on site that day and what they're doing. Typically, some of the key tasks that would fall to you are setting out any décor, laying finishing touches on your tables and possibly even laying out your tables. Planning what needs to be done and when will help make sure no time is wasted; for example, you can't put finishing touches to your tables until they've been laid out and the florist and marquee company have finished any work to be done to the ceiling.

I'd recommend having a team of willing helpers who are prepared to get their hands dirty and help you with your finishing touches. Just make sure you're realistic about what needs doing and how long it's likely to take you.

There are some tasks that will need to be done on the morning of your wedding, which include the following:

- Laying out any paper wedding stationery (for example, menus or place cards).
- Placing your flowers – this will most likely not be done until the actual day, because marquees can get very warm in the summer, and the flowers will quickly wilt.
- Putting out anything that is sweet (even if it's in wrappers) – believe me, those ants can smell it a mile off and will infest a wrapped sweet treat quicker than you can blink! And that's not something you want to clean up on the morning of your wedding day.
- Setting out any food and putting out the cake.
- Getting the drinks on ice.
- Doing a quick hoover, and removing any carpet coverings (if you have them).
- Checking the generator and making sure there's enough fuel.

Pro tip: A note on glasses: don't leave these upside down on tables overnight, as condensation will form in them and they'll look pretty grotty when your guests sit down. Ideally, place these on the tables on the morning of your wedding; the worst-case option is to do so the day before, but placing them the right way up.

Section 3

DESIGNING YOUR MARQUEE

R♥M
08 · 09 · 2018
EDDING · POST

Your Wedding Design

I imagine there is a good chance that the first thing you did once that question had been popped was to head straight to Pinterest and start pinning some inspirational images of how you wanted your day to look. However, wedding design is far more than pulling together inspiration and creating Pinterest boards; you need to be able to communicate your vision to your suppliers, create something personal to you both, and also let the suppliers' skills shine through.

Begin by thinking about your priorities and what you both like. Your marquee design will only be one element of your whole day, and it genuinely makes such a difference if you're able to thread your wedding design through all the different elements of your day.

You should brainstorm, read wedding blogs, seek inspiration in current trends, dig deep into what makes you both a unique couple and follow some aspirational wedding suppliers on Instagram. Once you've spread your net wide, you should start to see some commonalities among what you like (and dislike) – this is where you start with creating your design.

Assuming you've now curated some specific Pinterest boards or a mood board of your own to represent your wedding vision, then you need to blend those into the design for your marquee.

Zoning Your Marquee Space

Zoning is a way of dividing up the space within your marquee and making sure you maximise the space available inside. You need to think about how you want your day to run and how you're going to use the space. With a marquee, you have one huge expanse of space – particularly with clear span marquees and traditional pole marquees – which you'll need to transform into a workable wedding space. With a wedding, so much thought and care goes into how it'll look, that treating the whole of the marquee the same and as one large area doesn't really do it justice. Unlike a party, where you can have one open space for the whole event, this will be a day-long affair, so splitting your marquee into zones is a really useful way of maximising your space, creating a wow factor and creating a flow of events throughout the day.

So if we think about how a typical wedding day runs, you start with the ceremony, move on to reception drinks and canapés, then have the wedding breakfast and speeches, and this is followed by cutting the cake, the first dance, the evening food and the evening's entertainment. It's completely possible to use the one marquee to move your guests from the formality of the ceremony all the way through to the fun and frivolity of the evening.

The largest space allocation will be for the wedding breakfast, where you'll need to accommodate seating for all your guests, so the likelihood is that this area will also take up the largest part of your décor budget.

Annexes can be used to create different rooms.

Lighting can be used to zone specific areas.

Thinking through the logistics of where your guests will move from and to for each of these stages of your day will help you work out which areas of your marquee you'll need to segment off and how you'll do that. When your guests arrive in your marquee, do you want them to be greeted by some sort of entrance with a coat rail, somewhere to leave their gifts and somewhere to receive a drink, and to be able to see where they're going to be seated? Basically, unlike with a bricks-and-mortar venue – which would have a foyer, a bar, a restaurant and a dance room – you'll need to create these spaces yourself.

Here are some of my top tips for creating the zones:

» A reveal curtain can be hung across the width of the marquee.

» Furniture can be positioned within a specific part of the marquee to create a cosy seating area or to separate areas in a more casual way than having a full, floor-to-ceiling reveal curtain.

» Garden trellis can be decorated and used as a screen to section off areas.

» Trees and tall floral arrangements can be positioned to create entrances inside your marquee that will transition guests from one part of your day to another.

» Lighting can also be used to zone areas. Whether you'd like different coloured uplighters to divide the space up or simply put a black star cloth above the dance floor, this can be a less structural way of creating that flow and a way that also doesn't require any intervention as the day progresses.

» Adding annexes to your marquee can create different rooms; for example, one for a bar area or one for evening food. (Image designed using Marquee Tech software.)

Styling Your Marquee

The first thing that's going to dictate the styling of your marquee is the type you've selected. Tipis will need very little extra décor, and their structure will lend itself to lighting inside, whether this is strings of fairy lights, mounted spotlights or uplighters with different coloured gels. With marquees such as clear span or traditional-style ones, you'll have one large open space to play with, which will need a little more creativity.

Wedding breakfast

As I mentioned previously, the main part of your day that your marquee will be used for is your wedding breakfast, so the biggest decision with regard to styling your marquee will be what sort of tables you'll have. Will you have long, rustic-style tables or cloth-covered round tables? What style of chairs will you have? Given that this is where a large part of your day will be spent, it's definitely worth considering apportioning a significant part of your budget to this.

You'll also need to think about what's going on your tables. I'm a complete sucker for a beautiful tablescape. Pulling together the cutlery, crockery, glassware, table stationery, linens, florals and candles on a table to create an overall effect that ties in with your wedding design is so much fun! But do remember to consider what your catering team need and how much space on the table your food service will require.

Signage

As you're creating an event space from scratch that no one will have experienced before, it's a great idea to include some signage to help your guests navigate their way around. Again, think about the journey your guests will make from the moment they arrive. Will they have found the location from a postcode, or is there a hard-to-find entrance off a road? If so, consider having something there to signpost guests. Is the location of the parking obvious? Is it easy to see where they'd find the entrance to the marquee? Once they're in the marquee, do you need to signpost the toilets or the way back to the parking, for example? Incorporating these signs into your overall design is a great way of creating a cohesive look.

Pick signage that works with your wedding design:

Styling your marquee with colour

Given that you have a huge, white space, you'll need to consider injecting some colour into your styling. The traditional whites and greens will work, but if you have an ivory – or white -lined marquee – lean more towards the greens by including more foliage, otherwise you'll find the whites just blend in and it's a waste of your budget. Also consider that the canvas and linings on these marquees are not pure white, so all the colours you pick will have a yellow tone to them once positioned inside your marquee.

Another **top tip** is to consider using coloured linen on your tables or having exposed wooden tables, and choosing chairs that are not pure white. Adding a textured tablecloth in a subtle shade – even a soft grey – can completely lift the overall look. If coloured linen isn't your thing, then some simple, coloured candlesticks can be a cost-effective way of adding a design detail to your tables.

Another way of adding colour could be through putting little pops of it on your tables, using things such as stationery, napkins, water glasses or cutlery. Think about layering the colours and creating a colour palette with tones and textures to break up the expanse of white. Chairs can also be used to add texture and colour, whether you pick a coloured seat pad or some sort of chair decoration such as swags or bows.

If you want to get really into adding colour and create a more solid colour theme, you can introduce a coloured carpet, but be wary of this as it can become overpowering; a subtle charcoal or a neutral shade will be the most suitable in most cases, but definitely play around with it at the concept stage to see what you prefer. The other point to mention about carpets is that, believe it or not, people won't notice the carpet as long as it's unobtrusive. Your guests' eyes need to be drawn upwards not downwards to the carpet, so create your focal points at eye level and above.

Lighting your marquee

I often feel this is something that brides and grooms overlook, but lighting can make a massive difference to the overall style of your wedding marquee. I'd absolutely recommend that you put something in your budget for lighting inside your marquee. This can be as simple as swapping out the plain chandeliers and introducing something more grand, such as an oversized crystal chandelier for a glam look, or if you're more into a contemporary/urban look, then exposed Edison bulb displays are fabulous.

As well as the lights that hang down, also think about using lighting to create atmosphere. Having disco lighting when the music is on in the evening is quite obvious, but clever lighting can transition your wedding from day to evening and into the night. This could be uplighters that change colour to add interesting shades against the linings; fairy lights to add a twinkly sparkle in the evening; or a romantic, black, pea-lit cloth over your dance floor to help create your dancing zone.

Also think about candlelight. Check whether your marquee company and also your linen company are happy for you to use these first (sometimes they ban you from using real candles unless they're enclosed, as they can stain the tablecloths), but tea lights, pillar candles, tall candlesticks and candelabras can all add a romantic and intimate air to your dining tables. You can also buy really great replica candles (which are light-emitting diode [LED] lights), so you can explore that option if your marquee company won't permit the use of open flames.

Hanging festoon lights to criss-cross over your marquee ceiling is great if you're looking for a more fun alternative to hanging chandeliers, and you can even complement these with draping. This is particularly useful if you don't like the look of the standard pleated linings of your marquee, or if you have a traditional marquee and you want to lower the internal roof height to make it cosier.

Freestanding light-up letters make for a great focal point!

Bang on trend at the moment are neon signs, which can cast a colourful hue into your marquee and also add a bit of personalisation to your day.

There are so many options to explore, but your marquee company should be able to help you or you could go to a specific event-lighting company for some inspiration. My top advice would be to dedicate some of your wedding budget to this aspect of styling your wedding marquee.

DECORATING THE INSIDE OF YOUR MARQUEE

Chances are that you probably won't have a hard and fast theme for your wedding, but there will be little touches you want to inject into your day to make it feel cohesive and well thought out.

Flowers are the big thing here, and small jam jars on tables just won't give you the impact. You can use flowers in so many ways, whether it's having them on your tables, as hanging installations, or as garlands draping across the ceiling or round the perimeter. Introducing flowers and foliage really brings the outside in, which I think is where marquees really come into their own. Ensure you make use of your florist to really get to grips with any hanging installations, as these will need to be planned and executed properly due to the health and safety implications.

As I mentioned before, do think about which colours will show up well in your marquee; using bigger-headed flowers will give more impact and fill the space better. Also consider using foliage and flowers that have a scent, as this will make your whole marquee smell divine.

You may want to hire trees to break up your expanse and zone the areas within your marquee. Trees are also great for adding texture and warmth into your marquee; you can decorate them with twinkly lights to personalise them and bring them more in line with the rest of your design. Remember, though, there are some great artificial options available to hire, which can be more budget friendly (just check the height of your trees against the ceiling height in the part of your marquee where you want to stand them).

FOCAL POINTS IN YOUR MARQUEE

ONE OF THE ABSOLUTELY KEY THINGS FOR STYLING A MARQUEE IS TO KEEP YOUR DECORATIONS AT EYE LEVEL AND ABOVE. YOU WANT YOUR GUESTS TO ENTER AND LOOK UP. IF YOU SPEND SOME OF YOUR BUDGET ON SMALL BITS THAT SIT ON THE FLOOR, IT'LL JUST BE A WASTE.

When budget is a consideration, go bold: have fewer larger floral displays or prop displays. I'd also include tableware and table decorations in this bracket – think place cards, menus, knives, forks, etc. If budget is a consideration, then control your costs here – and I hate to say this because I love a beautifully dressed wedding table and gorgeous wedding stationery, but your budget has to come first!

Using focal points cleverly in your layout will definitely make your budget stretch further. Think about where you place these focal points too. Use them to create a flow around your marquee, incorporating the key events on your timeline. For example, think about cutting the cake – this is a prime photo opportunity, but so often the cake is displayed in a dark corner on a small, white table with a plain background. If you're spending money on a beautifully created cake, then consider showing this investment off as well as you can. Even if you need to get someone to move some of the freestanding décor around to create a better backdrop for your cake, then it'll be worth it when you receive your pictures! Spending money on your focal areas will also help you to stay focused during your planning; unless you have a massive budget and a huge team of volunteers, you can't do everything!

Draw your guests' eyes up for maximum impact.

Creating larger focal points is more budget savvy.

Which areas should you style?

Here are some key areas in your marquee to think about styling (though you may not have all these):

» Marquee entrance

» Ceiling space

» Dining tables

» Cake table/background

» Location for the speeches

» Gift table

» Casual-seating area

» Dance floor – think about those all-important first-dance pictures!

» Evening-food location

» Bar area

One final tip...

I know you'll have put so much thought, effort and budget into making your marquee look amazing, so don't forget to tell your photographer and videographer all the details! If you don't tell them the important bits you want to get photographed/videoed, there's a chance they'll get missed with all the other fun stuff happening!

Carve out 15 minutes of your photographer's time before your guests arrive (ideally before the bottles of wine get set out). This will allow them to take some wide-angled shots of the interior, capture that wow factor before everyone enters and moves the chairs and table decorations around, and record some of the finer details you have created!

Floral Installations

I'm asked by so many of my clients to plan a hanging floral installation within their marquee design, so I thought I'd explain a bit more about them and how you achieve them.

One of the key tricks with planning a successful marquee is to raise your guests' attention above eye level. Focusing your budget on fewer larger and more eye-catching displays is a budget-savvy way of creating the biggest impact for less money. Hanging floral installations are a great way of achieving this because they break up the roof line, and they add interest and texture. Having floral installations is a massive trend right now; are you going to have one?

Here's a step-by-step guide on what you need to know about hanging floral displays inside your marquee.

Collate Your Inspiration

To start with, get your inspiration together. Find pictures of different hanging installations on Pinterest or on wedding blogs. Gather examples of the size, shape and style of hanging floral installation you like. Don't worry too much at this stage about getting the exact image of the correct flowers, colours and foliage. Collect a variety of images, because you can then combine different ideas to get the perfect installation for you.

Styles of Hanging Floral Installations

The style and shape of the hanging floral installation you can have will very much depend on the type of marquee you've picked. Clear span marquees are easy to hang a variety of different types of installations in. The aluminium framework running throughout the length and width of it offers many hanging points. Traditional and sailcloth marquees have central poles, around or between which you can suspend floral installations. Tipis have their wooden framework, which again is fairly easy to hang floral installations from.

There are several different types of floral installations, and here are descriptions of some to give you some inspiration.

A floral chandelier

These can hang from the centre of the marquee or around a pole. They're usually built around a base, such as a hula hoop or a wooden frame. The lighter the frame, the better, because the florist will need to wire on the foliage and the flowers.

The main weight will be the water the flowers need to be kept in. There are a couple of options for this: mini test-tubes filled with water into which the stems are inserted, or oasis / floristry foam soaked in water. The oasis option is far heavier.

These can be made to look free-flowing and organic with trailing foliage/twigs or ribbons, or they can be more structured with a dense collection of flowers.

> Another **top tip** if you're hoping for lots of flowers in the chandelier is to opt for fake flowers rather than real ones. This way, they can be wired onto the frame, with no need for water/oasis, which is much lighter. I know that real flowers smell amazing, but believe me, with the height the chandelier will hang from, you'd have to be pretty clued-up to spot the difference, and the logistics will be far easier.

A floral ball

This is exactly the same as a chandelier, but on a ball-shaped base rather than on a ring. As with the chandelier, these can be densely packed with flowers or be a more organic shape with trailing foliage to give a more teardrop-shaped silhouette.

Floral chandeliers can hang from the apex in a clear span marquee.

Or between the two king poles in a traditional marquee.

You can also hang paper lanterns for some pops of colour.

Garlands

A garland is a string of sections of foliage wired together to make one long strand. These can be interspersed with wired-in flowers. You need to be mindful of the length of the garland versus the length of each foliage section, as you don't want the weight to cause sections to come undone once they've been hung up.

These can look stunning when intertwined with fairy lights and hung to follow the draping of the marquee roofline.

> It's also easy to echo the garland look on the table tops to create a cohesive look. Garlands also look great when strung between poles or around the circumference of the marquee walls.

Clouds

Clouds are similar to a ball, but less spherical. They're a more natural shape. Usually, they have a softer style of floral base, such as gypsophila or pampas grass. They can be created with ombre shading for something really unusual and romantic.

Hanging frames

These could be anything from a hanging ladder through to a larger shape. You make the frame and then cover it with your flowers and foliage. Another popular shape is a circle that hangs vertically rather than horizontally.

Hanging stems

Hanging individual stems is a really elegant way of adding something to the ceiling of your marquee. Although this looks really simple, it can be a bit of a challenge as the flowers don't sit in water. The installation needs to be done fairly last minute and has a whole heap of logistical challenges, so planning is imperative. You also need to pick robust stems that can be wired and won't wilt easily. It's also not a cheap option, as you need considerably more flowers because you won't be able to pad this out with foliage.

Planning Your Floral Installation

My biggest piece of advice for you here is to coordinate with all the suppliers involved. You'll need the input of the marquee company to check the fixings and the weight loading. The florist will have to be in the communication loop to confirm these details with the marquee company. I'd also recommend that you think about your caterers too and your deliveries. You don't want the installation to be happening when you're having the tables laid. Planning the installation when there's minimal activity in the marquee can help. Giving your florist some space and time to do their thing will cause less stress to all involved.

The floral installation will need to be one of the first things put into the marquee after it's been erected. Then the tables and chairs can be set out, followed by all the décor and pretty bits. The same also applies to the removal: do it all in reverse and don't try to take the hanging floral arrangements down before you've removed the tables. These logistics will need fine-tuning to make sure everything runs smoothly and all the suppliers dovetail their services into each other's.

From an engineering perspective, think about not only how the floral arrangement will hang but also how you'll get access to that height. For example, ask if the marquee company will install a pulley system for your florist. The florist can then work at chest height and raise the floral installation up into position once they're finished. Otherwise, you may need to consider hiring a cherry picker or a ladder system for your florist.

Speak in detail with your florist about your flower choices. Robust flowers that don't wilt easily and that need limited water are ideal. The same applies to the foliage, but be guided by their expertise and experience.

USING A FLORIST AND A MARQUEE COMPANY THAT HAVE EXPERIENCE OF SUCH INSTALLATIONS WILL DEFINITELY MAKE THIS PROCESS A LOT SMOOTHER FOR YOU.

Music for Your Wedding

Music sets the tone and vibe of your day, whether you're looking for something soothing for the background while your guests are being entertained with reception drinks and canapés, or something to really get the party started later in the evening. It's also a great way to help signpost the events of the day for your guests.

With a marquee, you'll need to consider the space you allocate to your musicians and what they will require to be able to provide their service.

Some typical requirements that you'll find on musicians' contracts may be these:

- Space for loading and unloading their equipment, and a designated parking spot.
- Somewhere for them to change (aka a green room).
- A safe space for them to store their cases/belongings.
- Refreshments and somewhere to sit between sets. Depending on the time of day they're performing, they may ask for a plated hot meal.
- A power supply with the correct number of sockets for their instruments.

- » Seats for use while playing.
- » A wet-weather plan if you're expecting them to play outside at any point.
- » Shade if they're playing outside in hot weather.

When I book musicians, I always mention that it'll be a marquee wedding, so they'll understand that weather is likely to play a part, they'll be using a temporary power supply, and they may not be playing on a hard surface. That way, if this is likely to pose a problem for them, they can explain the issues, and then plans can be put in place accordingly.

If you're holding your wedding on private property, then you aren't likely to have sound limiters; however, if your marquee is part of a venue, then this may well be something you need to consider. Sound limiters are electronic systems linked to your band's PA system that automatically cut off all amplified sound if it hits a predetermined decibel level. This is to prevent the music becoming too loud and infringing on any environmental restrictions or your TEN. Do speak to your venue coordinator and make sure you understand more about this, and then ensure that your musicians are fully aware of this.

As well as sound limiters, there are likely to be restrictions on the time by which you'll need to finish the music. Remember that the sound live bands emit is louder than from a DJ, so you may wish to plan your timings accordingly, and some venues will allow canned music to continue for longer than live music. Alternatively, you may wish to consider switching to a silent disco to avoid this problem completely! There are so many options for creating a lively atmosphere and getting everyone up and dancing; maybe you could even consider hiring a jukebox so your guests are in control of the playlist!

Some bands will bring their own lighting or smoke machines to create a complete experience for your guests, so it's definitely worth checking what equipment they have, how much space it all takes up (in terms of floor space) and what power it all requires. The last thing you want is for the band to lose power and lighting part way through a set, so you'll need to go into this in detail with them. If you're worried about power, then I'd highly recommend having a backup source, whether that's a second generator or a way of drawing from the mains supply at your venue.

Another question to ask is whether your band require any staging. If you're spending the bulk of your budget on a live band, and it's really important to you, then a stage maybe necessary. Your marquee company can help you with this, but double check the size with your band or their agent. A stage is also really useful if you don't have hard flooring in your marquee, as it means they have a solid surface to stand their instruments on.

Check if your band require a stage.

Allow time in your plans for any sound checks.

Music can really set the mood.

Bands and DJs should also come with their fully up-to-date public liability insurance documents and portable appliance testing (PAT) certificates. Some venues will ask to have copies of these for their files in advance of your wedding, so make sure that asking for them is on your checklist.

When you sign the contract for your musician or DJ, be sure to check their rider. This is a list of requirements, and it includes things such as refreshments, changing-room requirements, set timings, parking requirements and unloading/loading information. It'll be your contractual obligation to make sure that all these are provided to the band's satisfaction. If there are any that you may not be able to cater for, then have the conversation with the band before you sign the contract, so you can work out a compromise.

If you're having speeches, you may wish to use a PA system (with a microphone). Speak to your band before you hire one, because if they're there early enough for your speeches, some bands/DJs are happy to lend you theirs.

This brings me on to the subject of soundchecks and setting up. Depending on how you've arranged your marquee, you may be in a situation where your dance floor is open to your dining area. In this case, you should check with your band/DJ what time they'll need for setting up, because you don't want them to arrive midway through your wedding breakfast! It can be worth asking them to come and set up earlier in the day, especially if they're local. It may incur an extra charge, but it will definitely keep things neater. Alternatively, review your layout and see if you can screen off the band area so they can arrive and set up unseen.

Picking popular floor-fillers will get the dance floor packed!

Adding Luxury to Your Wedding

The word 'luxury' is usually associated with cost, but I think it's also about experience and every element being perfect. I also don't think it's just in relation to visual impact; those luxury touches cover everything from taste through to scents, sounds and sights.

Taste

I always think food and drink is one of the key areas that your guests will remember; that is, how well they were fed and watered. To be luxurious, the food doesn't need to be a plated, three-course meal, but it does need to be high quality and freshly prepared. Picking a caterer who has loads of experience of creating fine dining from a catering tent is really important, so make sure you ask them lots of questions and do masses of research before you pay your deposit.

Also, think about the drinks you want to serve to your guests, and then get creative. Having a bespoke his-and-hers cocktail is a fun and inventive way to treat your guests and inject some personality into your event.

SCENT

Did you know there are perfume companies that can create you a signature fragrance for your wedding day? Now this really would be a luxurious touch! You could use it at your ceremony and then follow it through into your marquee to create cohesion. The evocative power of scent adds an additional memorable and unique element to your day.

If having your own scent created just for your wedding is a little out of budget, then I'd highly recommend going heavy on your flower budget! Work closely with your florist to incorporate highly scented blooms and foliage. Marquees are brought to life completely with creative and good-quality floristry, as the fragrances from fresh flowers really hit you as you enter and will instantly put smiles on your guests' faces.

SOUND

Reflect on using sound to provide the third luxurious touch for your marquee. Consider carefully how music will play its role in your day. It can create a mood and atmosphere, and it can guide your guests from one part of your day to the next. For example, an elegant string quartet playing outside your marquee during the reception is a lovely way to welcome your guests; it isn't so intrusive that it prevents the easy flow of conversation, but it is lively enough that it kicks off proceedings after the more formal 'I do's.

> WHAT ABOUT WHILE YOU'RE SEATED FOR YOUR WEDDING BREAKFAST? HAVING SOME MUSIC IN THE BACKGROUND CAN COMPLEMENT THE MENU YOU HAVE CHOSEN AND CAN HELP WITH THE PACE OF THE DINING EXPERIENCE.

As things move into the more lively part of your wedding, think about your music for the evening. There are so many options for this, whether you want to ease your guests into the dancing with a refined love song for your first dance, then have some popular songs to get people up and dancing, followed by some late-night dance music for those die-hard party-goers.

Pick a caterer with an eye for detail.

Using fresh flowers will fill the air with scent.

Luxurious details will enhance your guests' experience.

SIGHT

Finally, the most obvious luxury element of a marquee wedding is the design and how your wedding is styled. This is an area where luxury is in every detail, from your fabulous dress through to the cutlery with which your guests will be eating.

The interior of your marquee is going to be a huge part of creating a luxurious day for your wedding. Think fabulous linens, fine china, high-quality stationery, crystal glassware and amazing floral displays. For a marquee, keeping your flowers at eye level or above is critical. Hanging floral displays are bang on trend and look amazing. Not only do they give a fabulous scent but they also add colour and texture.

BEAUTIFULLY DESIGNED, PINTEREST-WORTHY TABLESCAPES WILL MAKE A HUGE IMPACT ON YOUR GUESTS AS THEY ENTER YOUR MARQUEE, WHICH MEANS IT REALLY IS WORTH SPENDING THE MONEY ON A SPECIALIST WEDDING PLANNER OR STYLIST WHO HAS A HIGH LEVEL OF ATTENTION TO DETAIL, SO AS TO REALLY MAKE SURE THE DESIGN IS PERFECTLY EXECUTED AND PERFECTLY ON POINT.

Other luxury touches to add are in the technical aspects of the structure. Adding a hard floor, integrating a cloakroom into the main marquee so that the toilet block is within the main marquee structure, adding annexes so your marquee is broken into zones, and using lighting and draping are all important design elements to consider, and Pinterest is great for getting inspiration for these finishing touches.

Of course, none of these extra flourishes will be worthwhile unless you have also invested in making sure everything is planned meticulously, which is where an experienced wedding planner can help. Having the input of a planner will add an extra layer of quality and finesse to your day, and it will only add to the experience you and your guests have.

What's Next?

I've packed as much of my real-life experience into this book as I could, so I hope I haven't bamboozled you too much! If your thought process and wedding planning follows what I've shared, then you'll find your planning to be calmer and more logical. Having structure to your planning and knowing some of the pitfalls that may lie ahead will hopefully allow you to enjoy this part of the process and get you excited about the build-up to your big day. I also believe that if you're equipped with as much knowledge as you can be beforehand, then you can trust the process more and lean into the creative details, which will really allow you to develop a unique and personal wedding that you'll cherish the memories of for many years to come.

I've covered a lot, so you can see just how complex it can be and all the different things you need to take into consideration, so if you feel like commissioning the services of an experienced planner who specialises in marquee weddings, then do drop me a message at **info@emilyandrewevents.co.uk** to see how I can help.

Just in case you missed any, here are the checklists you should have:

- » Marquee site assessment checklist
- » Portable toilet vanity kit checklist
- » DIY bar checklist
- » Marquee floor-plan checklist
- » Emergency kit checklist

For even more tips and advice come and follow me here:

Instagram – @emilyandrewevents

Facebook – @emilyandrewevents

Pinterest – @emilyandrewevents

Here are some links that will help you with your planning:

- » The UK Alliance of Wedding Planners (tips and advice on working with planners and for planning your own wedding): www.ukawp.com
- » MUTA (the UK's only industry standards organisation for marquee providers; you can search for its members): www.muta.org.uk
- » Coco Wedding Venues' directory (some ideas for marquee locations): cocoweddingvenues.co.uk/venue_feature/marquee-tipi/
- » English Wedding Blog (gorgeous English wedding inspiration): english-wedding.com
- » The Wedding Blueprint (the ultimate wedding-planning journal to keep your planning on track): theweddingblueprint.co.uk

GLOSSARY

Baffle screen – A staggered screen that is placed at the entrance of the catering tent where it joins the main marquee, which is used to prevent guests having a direct view into the kitchen area.

Canapé – A mouthful-sized piece of food that is usually served alongside an aperitif before your wedding breakfast.

Celebrant – An officiant who will lead your ceremony, but who isn't able to perform a legal ceremony in the UK.

Commission – A fee payable by wedding suppliers, usually to the venue the wedding is being held at, in acknowledgement of the business; this is generally a percentage on the final invoice the couple pay that supplier.

Contingency plan – An additional plan for your day (or part of your day) to take into account when things may go wrong (for example, if there's wet weather, if the band is delayed or if the speeches overrun).

Corkage – A fee paid to your venue or catering team per bottle when you supply your own alcohol.

Dry bar – A bar hired without staff, drinks or equipment.

Dry-hire venue – A wedding venue you hire that isn't fully equipped; that is, one where you have to hire in everything you need, from chairs and tables to music, etc.

Favours – Gifts given by the couple to each guest as a thank you for attending their wedding. Historically, they'd have been five sugar-coated almonds to represent fertility, longevity, wealth, happiness and health.

Festoon lights – Light-bulb-style outdoor or indoor lights.

Floral installation – A large floral arrangement (for example, a hanging flower arrangement, a large pedestal, an entrance arch or a flower wall).

Golden hour – The hour before sunset when the light has a golden quality to it, which is ideal for portraits of the happy couple.

Guy ropes – The ropes used to hold up a traditional, tipi, stretch or sailcloth-style marquee.

Master of ceremonies (or toastmaster) – This is a person who can coordinate timings, make important announcements during the wedding day, and add an air of formality and tradition to a wedding.

Panoramic windows – A PVC window panel that is all transparent to allow a clear view.

Reveal curtain – A partition across the width of your marquee to divide the space and enable an area to be revealed later in the proceedings.

Silent disco – A disco at which everyone on the dance floor wears wireless headphones and listens to dance music through them.

Tablescape – The whole design for your wedding-breakfast table (crockery, cutlery, glassware, table stationery, flowers, candles, chairs, linens, favours, etc.)

Wedding breakfast – The first meal you enjoy as a married couple; it can be at any time of the day.

Wedding coordinator – Someone who works behind the scenes to make sure your wedding runs smoothly; this is quite often an on-the-day specialist who isn't involved in all the planning in the lead up to creating a wedding.

Wedding planner – Someone who works closely with their clients as the interface between them and their suppliers, and who designs, plans and executes a wedding day.

SNAUWAERT